MURDER & MAYHEM
ON CHICAGO'S
NORTH SIDE

MURDER & MAYHEM
ON CHICAGO'S
NORTH SIDE

TROY TAYLOR

Charleston   London

THE
History
PRESS

Published by The History Press
Charleston, SC 29403
www.historypress.net

Copyright © 2009 by Troy Taylor
All rights reserved

Images are courtesy of the author unless otherwise noted.

First published 2009

Manufactured in the United States

ISBN 978.1.59629.644.2

Library of Congress Cataloging-in-Publication Data

Taylor, Troy.
Murder and mayhem on Chicago's North Side / Troy Taylor.
p. cm.
Includes bibliographical references.
ISBN 978-1-59629-644-2
1. Murder--Illinois--Chicago--History. 2. Crime--Illinois--Chicago--History. I. Title.
HV6534.C4T39 2009
364.152'30977311--dc22
2009005835

CONTENTS

Acknowledgements

I would like to thank Adam Selzer and Ken Berg for their always invaluable help with this book, as well as my friend John Winterbauer, who encouraged my passion for historic Chicago crime. Thanks also to the many writers and chroniclers of crime in the Windy City, especially Herbert Asbury, Jay Robert Nash and Richard Lindberg, and to the kind keepers of libraries, history rooms and archives who always went out of their way to help. Thanks also to Jonathan Simcosky at The History Press and to my wife, Haven, for always believing in me.

INTRODUCTION

C hicago is a city that was born in blood. The first settlers who came to the shores of Lake Michigan were brutally slaughtered during an Indian massacre, and even the man considered by many to be Chicago's founding father murdered another man during a land dispute. It was a gruesome start for a city that was already rooted in chaos.

Chicago was not planned in the way that other great American cities were. Its birthplace was not carefully chosen, and the streets were not laid out with care. Chicago began as nothing more than empty wilderness and open prairie, a desolate and isolated region on the shore of a great lake. The land on both sides of the Chicago River was low and wet, a brackish area of swamp and mud. A large portion of it spent part of the year under the murky waters of the lake. The mouth of the river itself was choked with sand, allowing passage of nothing larger than a canoe. The streambed was filled with rice and wild onions, an aromatic vegetable that would give Chicago its name—or perhaps not.

Nobody really knows for sure why the city was called Chicago. On the banks of the river grew wild onion—or perhaps it was garlic—which the Indians allegedly called *chickagou*. Some claim that the name of the city came from the Indian word *sheecaugo*, meaning "playful waters," or from the word *chocago*, meaning "destitute." Others suggest it came from the word *shegahg*, which meant "skunk," or from an Indian chief named Chicagou. And the list goes on. In general, though, most just interpreted the name to mean "bad smell," and for some reason, the moniker stuck.

Chicago went from being a spot on the map through which French explorers passed to an active settlement in the early 1800s. By this time, America was expanding its borders, and settlers, trappers, traders and soldiers came to the region, establishing a small settlement and a frontier outpost called Fort Dearborn.

Introduction

In 1804, a man named John Kinzie arrived in the region. He bought out the property of Jean Lalime and, over the course of several years, became the self-appointed civilian leader of the settlement. He was known for his sharp dealings with the local Indians over trade goods and furs. He also established close ties with the Potawatomi Indians and even sold them liquor, which created tension among the other settlers. Kinzie managed to become very successful, and this seemed to anger Jean Lalime, the man who had sold Kinzie his business. The two became bitter rivals, and eventually the hard feelings boiled over into violence when Lalime was stabbed to death.

Once that blood was spilled, it seemed that Chicago acquired a taste for it.

In August 1812, tension erupted into violence on the Illinois frontier. War had broken out once more between America and Great Britain, and the conflict had created unrest among the local Indian tribes, namely the Potawatomis and their allies who had hard feelings toward the American settlers. The commander at Fort Dearborn was ordered to evacuate the outpost, and while journeying to Fort Wayne in Indiana, the majority of the company—men, women and children alike—was massacred on the shores of Lake Michigan.

Chicago may have gotten off to a bloody start, but actual crime came slowly to the region. The first Chicago settlers were a rough lot, but there was no record of criminal activity in the area until the first population boom of the early 1830s. Thousands swarmed into the region from the east, and among these was Chicago's first thief. In addition, the mob of new arrivals brought the first man to be housed in the city jail. This drifter, known only as "Harper," was apparently arrested in the early fall of 1833 as a vagrant. Thanks to Illinois law at the time, vagrants could be offered for sale into slavery. Public sentiment was opposed to the sale of a white man, and even though a large crowd attended the auction, the only bid came from George White, a black man who was employed as the town crier. Harper was sold to him for a quarter, and White led him away at the end of a chain. What became of Harper after that is unknown, but it's thought that he escaped that night and quickly fled the city.

The name of Chicago's first thief has never been recorded, but he reportedly stole thirty-four dollars from a fellow boarder at the Wolf Tavern. Constable Reed arrested him, and the missing funds were discovered when the man was taken to Reed's carpentry shop and ordered to strip. The money was found wadded up in the toe of one of the man's socks. The defendant was held over for trial, which took place at the tavern, and after much argument and speech-making, he was found guilty. He was released on a nominal bail, pending a motion for a new trial by his boisterous attorney, Giles Spring, and he promptly disappeared.

By the late 1830s, Chicago newspapers were publishing an increasing number of accounts detailing thefts, holdups, drunken disturbances, street brawls and small riots. Other cities began to notice, and in the summer of 1839, a newspaper in Jackson, Michigan, commented that the "population of Chicago is principally composed of dogs and loafers."

One of these "loafers" was a young Irishman named John Stone who went to the gallows and became the first legal execution in Chicago history. Stone arrived in America at the age of thirteen and came to Chicago in 1838, after having served prison time for robbery and murder in Canada. He worked off and on as a woodcutter but spent most of his time in saloons and in the city's first billiard hall. In the spring of 1840, Stone was arrested for the rape and murder of Mrs. Lucretia Thompson, the wife of a Cook County farmer. In May, he was tried and convicted of the crime. On Friday, July 10, Stone was taken by wagon to a spot on the lakeshore about three miles south of the courthouse. About two hundred mounted citizens and sixty armed militiamen, under the command of Colonel Seth Johnson, escorted him to the gallows. He was hanged in front of a large crowd of interested spectators, and after his death, his body was taken by Doctors Boone and Dyer and dissected for medical study.

Even from these early days, Chicago thrived on its reputation for being a "wide-open town." As far back as the 1850s, the city gained notoriety for its promotion of vice in every shape and form. It embraced the arrival of prostitutes, gamblers, grifters and an outright criminal element. A commercialized form of vice flourished during the Civil War era, and it is believed that an estimated thirteen hundred prostitutes roamed the dark streets of Chicago. Randolph Street was lined with bordellos, wine rooms and cheap dance halls, and the area became known as "Gambler's Row," mostly because a man gambled with his very life when braving the streets of this seedy and dangerous district.

The Great Fire of 1871 swept away the worst of the city's vice areas, destroying both gin rooms and disease-ridden prostitution cribs, but a desire for illicit activities caused it to rebound quickly. By the 1880s, Chicago had gained its place as a mature city and also as a rail center for the nation. Waves of foreigners and immigrants poured into the city, and with the arrival of the World's Fair in 1893, thousands of new citizens followed.

During the latter part of the 1800s, random street crimes became the bane of Chicago's citizens. It became a good general rule for residents and visitors to avoid all but the busiest thoroughfares at night. Many places were

The Great Chicago Fire wiped out the worst of the gin rooms and disease-infested houses of prostitution, but the vice districts rebounded quickly and Chicago became known once again as a "wide-open town." *Courtesy of* Harper's Weekly.

considered unsafe after dark, and the lack of well-lighted streets in many areas added to the danger. It was suggested to travelers that they might always consider walking in the center of the street if possible. That way, they would be out of reach of any holdup man who might step out of an alley. Weapons among the criminal element could mean anything from a club to a knife to a canvas bag filled with sand or a pistol. As there were no laws in those days against concealed weapons, any drifter or drunk who got hold of a pistol could become a deadly menace. The thief may have only been looking for a little cash or some jewelry, but his "harmless" crime could easily become murder with a gun involved.

Not all of the crimes in Chicago were carried out at the wrong end of a gun—some of them were carried out in the smoke-filled backrooms of Chicago politics. In a town where the most popular slogan on election day was "vote early and vote often," political hijinks were just about guaranteed. It was just that sort of underhanded manipulation that almost sabotaged what we think of today as Chicago's famous North Side.

Since 1835, a large portion of the city's North Side had been used as a cemetery. Its existence had effectively halted the growth of the downtown business district and an expanding residential area, stalling development of anything north of Fullerton Avenue for many years. That changed in 1865, when an alderman named Lawrence Proudfoot was elected to the city council. The cemetery was already a hotly debated subject among city politicians, who had already succeeded in removing and relocating many of those buried in the cemetery to other places, hoping to cash in on the real estate frenzy that was sure to come. Proudfoot, Chicago's newest alderman, had other ideas for the land. He planned to get the sixty acres of ground set aside as a public park, making the necklace of green islands something that all Chicagoans could enjoy.

Proudfoot took the proposal to the state capital in Springfield after the rest of the city council rallied the troops and voted down his plan. The state legislators stood up to the Chicago politicians, supported Proudfoot and established the North Park Commission in February 1865. A wide swath of land, which extended north of Oak Street Beach to Montrose Avenue, was reserved for public use. By playing one band of politicians against another, the Chicago alderman helped create Lincoln Park, which opened in 1868. Proudfoot, although new to the Chicago political game, understood the

Lake Shore Drive and Lincoln Park, 1905. *Courtesy of the Detroit Publishing Co.*

backroom dealings of both city and state bosses, especially those in Chicago, who would go on to earn a reputation for unchecked plunder and graft.

The establishment of Lincoln Park led to massive development on the North Side. However, in those days, only small, remote towns existed on the other side of the park. They were part of the Lake View Township, which had been incorporated in 1857 and was bounded by Fullerton, Western and Devon Avenues and the Lake Michigan shoreline. Lake View included villages like Roseville, Summerdale, Andersonville, Rose Hill, Gross Park and Belle Plaine, and when it was swallowed up by the city in 1889, it became the Lake View neighborhood. Today, there is Old Lake View and East Lake View, which includes New Town, Buena Park, Uptown and Wrigleyville.

A traveler who ventured beyond Lake View in the decades after the Civil War only encountered a few farmhouses on what was mostly empty land. Uptown, at the north end of Lake View, was sparsely populated and was an ideal hideout for outlaws and bandits. The search for Dr. Patrick Cronin, the Irish nationalist who was abducted the same year that Lake View was absorbed by Chicago, brought detectives to this countryside, and his body was pulled from a catch basin at what are now Foster and Broadway.

Dr. Cronin was a well-to-do medical practitioner with an office at 1225 North Clark Street when he vanished in 1889. In addition to being a respected doctor, he was also a part of the secret Clan-Na-Gael Society, which was dedicated to freeing Ireland from British rule. However, Cronin was a moderate, opposed to the more radical elements of the clan that plotted terrorist bombings in Great Britain. He often spoke out against the militant factions, which led to him being expelled from the organization and accused of conspiring with British agents to disrupt the clan's efforts. There was no truth to the accusations, but members of the clan voted him guilty anyway and set his punishment as death. A police detective from the East Chicago Avenue station named Dan Coughlin drew the lot to carry out his execution.

Cronin vanished soon after, and only a few traces of blood and clumps of hair were left in his wake. About three weeks later, on May 23, 1889, his naked body was found floating in murky water when sewer workers checked a clogged catch basin about three hundred yards from the Argyle Park Station of the Chicago & Evanston branch of the Chicago, Milwaukee & St. Paul Railroad.

The investigation into his murder was led by Inspector Michael Schaak. Schaak harbored deep hostility toward the Irish immigrants who had settled among the Germans on the city's North Side. He ordered the arrest and interrogation of several hundred suspects, all of whom were mostly involved

Dr. Patrick Henry Cronin was murdered at a time of great Irish nationalism in Chicago in 1889. *Courtesy of the* Chicago Daily News.

with, or sympathetic to, the cause of Irish freedom. With physical evidence from the crime, which included medical reports and items found at the Lake View cottage where Cronin was murdered, a grand jury returned indictments against the inner circle of the Clan-Na-Gael.

Amidst charges of jury tampering and bribery, the first Cronin murder trial ended on December 16, 1889, with several guilty verdicts, including one for triggerman Dan Coughlin. He immediately appealed the verdict and was granted a new trial. The testimony remained the same the second time around, but the verdict was different—the detective was acquitted on March 8, 1894. He was greeted by a large crowd of enthusiastic supporters when he left the courthouse, and he spent the remainder of his days as a Chicago saloonkeeper.

The entire affair was a blight on the Chicago justice system and the start of a bad reputation for the city's North Side.

By the start of the twentieth century, the quiet areas of Uptown, Edgewater and Rogers Park were on their way to becoming affluent residential areas for the wealthy. The availability of land and the Northwestern Elevated Line, which began operations in 1900, started a commercial and residential building boom, turning what had been open fields into homes, streets and businesses. The Germans and the Scandinavians formed ethnic pockets on the North Side, establishing neighborhoods, community centers and churches.

The addition of hotels and high-rise apartments along Sheridan Road brought even more people to the area, as did the establishment of Essanay Studios on West Argyle Street. The movie studio was founded in Uptown by George K. Spoor and "Bronco Billy" Anderson, the *S* and *A* of Ess-an-ay. The studio's first film, *An Awful Skate, or The Hobo on Rollers*, starred Ben Turpin, who was then the studio's janitor. It was produced for only $200 but managed to gross several thousand dollars when it was released. Essanay soon prospered, and movie performers soon began flocking to Chicago.

At that time, filmmakers were abandoning the East Coast, hoping to stay one step ahead of the stringent copyright rules that had been imposed on the fledgling industry by Thomas Edison. Chicago was just far enough west to stay under the radar, at least for a while. Essanay produced silent films with up-and-coming and future stars like Wallace Beery, Francis X. Bushman, Gloria Swanson, cowboy star Tom Mix, Edward Arnold and, of course, former janitor Ben Turpin. The Uptown neighborhood became home to the stars and the site of many location shots. The nearby Chicago & Western railroad tracks along Ravenswood were often featured in *The Perils of Pauline* cliffhangers, and Castlewood Terrace became a one-block forerunner to

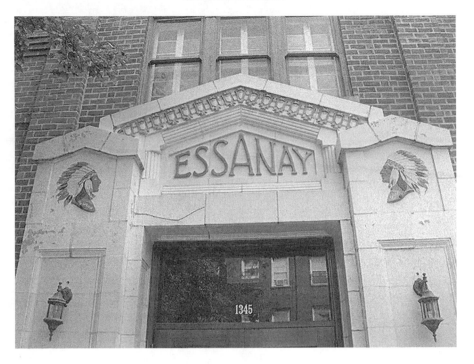

The front entrance to the old Essanay Studios on Chicago's North Side.

Beverly Hills. Essanay's films took the public by storm, but eventually the unpredictable nature of Chicago's weather led to the company relocating to the new movie capital of California. The studio survived until 1925, although the buildings in Chicago still remain today.

The arrival of the movie crowd sparked the development of Uptown as an entertainment and nightclub district—and it also attracted gangsters to the North Side. The transient film and vaudeville workers who lived in the myriad apartments in the lakefront neighborhoods, the song and dance men, chorus girls, comics and musicians all combined to make Uptown and Lake View irresistible to Chicago mobsters. The North Side became not only a place where Prohibition booze could be peddled, but it also became a great hideout for gangsters on the run. The faceless apartments, gin mills and dance spots managed to keep these hoodlums out of sight and highly entertained. John Dillinger, members of the Barker-Karpis gang and their scores of imitators drifted in and out of the North Side at their leisure, rarely bothered by local law enforcement. It wasn't until someone tipped off the feds that they had to pull up stakes and head for the next town.

INTRODUCTION

The Uptown nightclubs like the Aragon Ballroom and the Green Mill, which were frequented by gangsters, also lured Chicagoans of modest means. Such places promised an escape from the drudgery of daily life and the hardships of the Depression. The nightclubs offered excitement, jazz and late-night dancing under the stars. But in order to satisfy the demands of the people who came to the clubs in search of a stiff drink, the Prohibition mobs of the 1920s were forced to battle it out with one another. The battles often ended in bloodshed and death, carried out in places all over the city. But there was no location as infamous as an out-of-the-way garage on North Clark Street, where the most brutal mass murder in Chicago's gangland history took place on St. Valentine's Day 1929.

THE ST. VALENTINE'S DAY MASSACRE

The rise of organized crime in Chicago began with the advent of Prohibition. The law that banned the sale and production of liquor went into effect in 1920, and lawless elements in the city began to make vast fortunes. The decline of these criminal empires began almost a decade later, in February 1929. It was on St. Valentine's Day of that year that the general public no longer saw the mob as "public benefactors," offering alcohol to a thirsty city, but as the collection of killers and thugs that it truly was.

Of course, the St. Valentine's Day Massacre was not the death knell for the mob in Chicago. Organized crime remains in the city today, but it was this bloody event that changed the face of crime in Chicago forever. In the years that followed, empires crumbled and lives were destroyed, bringing an end to the "glory days" of the mob in the Windy City.

The story of the Chicago mob truly begins with one of the most important criminals in pre-Prohibition Chicago, Big Jim Colosimo. In addition to running a popular restaurant in the South Side Levee District, Colosimo was also an influential brothel keeper, and he kept close ties to a number of important city officials. In this way, he ensured his political clout and maintained his ability to operate his criminal enterprises without interference. By 1915, he was the acknowledged overlord of prostitution on the South Side.

While operating his string of whorehouses, Colosimo brought a young man named Johnny Torrio from New York to be his bodyguard and right-hand man. It would be Torrio's ambitions that would lead to Colosimo's violent death. In 1920, Torrio wanted to expand the business into bootlegging, but Colosimo had no interest in this. His lack of forward thinking led Torrio to order his murder on May 11, 1920. Colosimo was shot in the head in the lobby of his restaurant. Torrio took over Colosimo's

The body of Big Jim Colosimo was discovered in the lobby of his South Side restaurant. He was shot in the back of the head shortly before Johnny Torrio and Al Capone began their rise to the top of the Chicago underworld. *Courtesy of the* Chicago Daily News.

business and quickly went to work, using a friend from New York as his muscle. That young man's name was Alphonse Capone.

Capone was born in Brooklyn in 1899 and made a name for himself as a gunman with the famous Five Points gang in New York, of which several of his cousins were members. Capone was only twenty-three when he came to Chicago, but Torrio soon promoted him to the post of manager in one of his toughest dives, the Four Deuces on South Wabash Avenue. During his time at the Four Deuces, Capone became Torrio's first lieutenant and chief gunman. In those days, he was rough and brutal, and there was little to indicate that he was destined for criminal greatness in the years to come. In the underworld, he was generally known as "Scarface Al Brown," a nickname that came from the two parallel scars on his left cheek that had been left behind during a knife fight. Soon, however, all of Chicago would be familiar with his name.

Torrio and Capone moved up quickly after Colosimo's death. The gangs on the South Side quickly fell in line with their plans. Torrio's beer began to

The St. Valentine's Day Massacre

Mob boss Johnny Torrio. The scarf around his neck hides bullet wounds from an assassination attempt by the North Side mob. *Courtesy of the* Chicago Daily News.

flow, and it was distributed by local gangs on the South and West Sides of the city.

Up until 1922, the Chicago gangland remained at peace. Then, the South Side O'Donnells, led by Spike O'Donnell, decided to rise up against Torrio. They were massacred back into their place over a period of about two years, between 1923 and 1925. Not long after, the Genna brothers, who supplied Torrio with poorly made liquor that was manufactured in neighborhood stills, began to get greedy and demanded a larger piece of the action. Wars began to erupt, but most of the trouble seemed to come from the North Side mob, an eccentric legion of mostly Irish gunmen led by Dion O'Banion. The high-quality Canadian liquor that was sent to Torrio by the Purple Gang in Detroit was constantly being hijacked by the North Side mob. O'Banion also moved his bootlegging operation into Cicero, which Torrio and Capone had already staked out as their exclusive territory.

Chicago underworld kingpin Al Capone in 1930. *Courtesy of the* Chicago Daily News.

The St. Valentine's Day Massacre

Dean Charles O'Banion was born in 1892 in the small central Illinois town of Maroa. Dean spent the early years of his life in Maroa, but after the death of both his mother and sister, his family moved to Chicago. Dean (soon to be known as Dion) saw the end of his innocent years. O'Banion found himself turning to the streets for a playground. He became involved with a street gang known as the Little Hellions and began picking pockets and rolling drunks. At the same time, he sang in the choir at the Holy Name Cathedral and, on Sunday, served as an altar boy.

For a time, O'Banion worked as a singing waiter at the McGovern brother's café and saloon on North Clark Street, crooning and balancing a hefty tray of beer glasses. McGovern's was a rough place filled with crooks. It was here that O'Banion met, and befriended, notorious safecrackers and thieves like George "Bugs" Moran, Earl "Hymie" Weiss, Vincent "the Schemer" Drucci and Samuel "Nails" Morton. With these men at his side, O'Banion put together one of the most devastating gangs in Chicago. They centered their activities on the North Side, around the Lincoln Park neighborhood and the Gold Coast.

When Prohibition came along, O'Banion purchased several of the best breweries and distilleries on the North Side. While Capone and Torrio on the South Side were forced to import beer and whiskey at high prices, or rely on rotgut produced by the Gennas to supply their outlets, O'Banion had the finest beer and booze available.

All over the city, society people and the owners of better restaurants bought from O'Banion. The quality of his product was better, and it was thought that he was more trustworthy than Capone, who was also running brothels and floating gambling operations. O'Banion publicly agreed to keep his operations north of the "dividing line," or Madison Street, but still serviced his special customers on the South Side as well.

At first, this encroachment on Capone-Torrio territory was tolerated. Capone attempted to negotiate with him, stating that if O'Banion was going to run booze on the South Side, then Capone should be allowed to have liquor warehouses in Lincoln Park. O'Banion refused—not because he couldn't deal with Capone, but because he was morally offended by Capone's dealings in prostitution. However, O'Banion's religious compunctions did not apply to hijacking Capone's trucks, robberies, gambling casinos and the killing of anyone who got in his way.

Torrio constantly tried to negotiate with O'Banion rather than use the violence that Capone urged. Dozens of meetings were held between Torrio, Capone and the North Side gang, and each ended with the same results. O'Banion always promised to recognize Torrio's territory but never kept his

Dion O'Banion and his wife. The leader of the North Side mob was an ally of Torrio and Capone in the early days, but gang warfare led to his assassination in 1924. *Courtesy of the* Chicago Daily News.

word. However, Torrio knew that if he killed O'Banion, it would mean all-out war in Chicago.

His hesitation backfired on him in May 1924, when O'Banion came to him and told him that he planned to retire and wanted to sell Torrio his largest gambling den and his favorite brewery. Torrio agreed to buy up O'Banion's concerns and reportedly paid him half a million dollars in cash two days later. The gang leaders agreed to meet at the brewery on May 19, as Torrio wanted to inspect his new property. He had not been there for more than ten minutes before Police Chief Collins, leading twenty officers, raided the place and arrested O'Banion, Earl "Hymie" Weiss and Torrio. This was Torrio's second arrest for violating Prohibition. He had been arrested once and fined in June 1923, but a second arrest could mean jail time—a fact of which O'Banion had been very much aware. Torrio also realized that O'Banion had no intention of retiring. He had conned Torrio into buying a brewery that he knew the police were about to shut down.

Torrio decided that it was time to get rid of O'Banion. When Mike Merlo, the founder and president of the powerful Unione Siciliana died in November 1924, Torrio saw a way to kill the North Side gang leader. O'Banion was the owner of Schofield's Flower Shop, across the street from Holy Name Cathedral, which was known as the only place to buy flowers for gangland funerals. Torrio would have his enemy killed in his own place.

On November 10, James Genna and Carmen Vacco entered O'Banion's flower shop and ordered a wreath for Merlo's funeral. They gave O'Banion $750 to pay for the arrangement. They told him that they would send some boys back to pick it up a little later. They left the shop. Five minutes later, the telephone rang and an unknown caller wanted to know if O'Banion had the flowers ready. He promised they would be ready at noon, and at five minutes past the hour, a blue Jewett touring car pulled up in front of the shop.

One of the shop's employees, a black man named William Crutchfield, who was sweeping up flower petals in the back room, looked up to see three men get out of the car and walk into the shop. Another man remained at the wheel of the car outside. O'Banion, dressed in a long white smock and holding a pair of florist's shears in his left hand, came out from behind the counter and extended his hand in greeting. "Hello, boys," O'Banion greeted them. "You from Mike Merlo's?"

The three men walked abreast and approached O'Banion with smiles on their faces. The man in the center was tall, clean-shaven and wearing an expensive overcoat and fedora. It was determined years later that this man was Frankie Yale. The other two, believed to be John Scalise and Albert Anselmi, were shorter and stockier, with dark complexions.

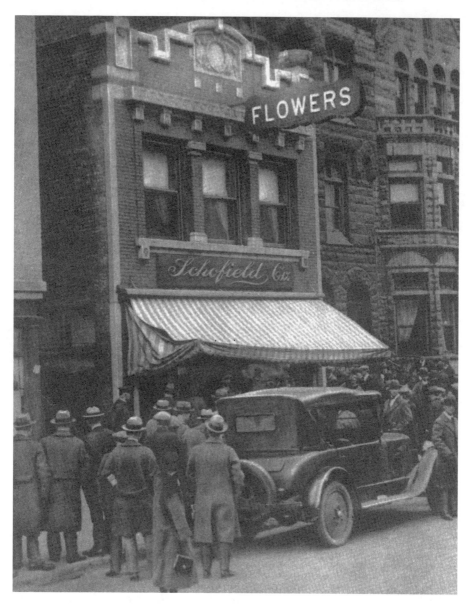

Schofield's Flower Shop in downtown Chicago, where Dion O'Banion was murdered by members of the Capone organization in November 1924. *Courtesy of the* Chicago Daily News.

"Yes, for Merlo's flowers," Crutchfield heard Frankie Yale say before he stepped closer to O'Banion. Yale grabbed the other man's hand in greeting and pulled O'Banion toward him. The two men at his sides moved around him and drew pistols. Then, at close range, Yale rammed his own pistol into

The St. Valentine's Day Massacre

O'Banion's stomach and, holding his arm in a vice-like grip, opened fire. All three men fired their weapons and the bullets ripped into O'Banion. Two slugs struck him in the right breast, two hit him in the throat and one passed through each side of his face. The shots were fired so close that powder burns were found at the opening of each wound. From that point on, this method of murder became known as the "Chicago Handshake."

O'Banion fell over dead, crashing into a display of geraniums. The three pistols that he had hidden on his body were unfired, not even drawn. The three men fled the store and climbed into the car outside, which drove slowly away from the scene.

The murder was never solved. No arrests were ever made and no one was ever indicted.

O'Banion's funeral was the most lavish in Chicago gangland history. The hearse was led to Mount Carmel Cemetery by twenty-six trucks filled with flowers worth more than $50,000. The scene at the cemetery was even more bizarre. On one side of the grave, lowering the body to rest, were Hymie Weiss, George Moran and Vincent Drucci; on the other, Al Capone, Johnny Torrio and Angelo Genna. There was no violence at the funeral—that was still to come.

As Torrio suspected, O'Banion's death ignited an all-out war in Chicago. A few days after O'Banion's funeral, in November 1924, Torrio and his wife

George "Bugs" Moran, shown here with his wife, took over as the leader of the North Side mob after the death of Dion O'Banion. He became known as the "man who got away" after his near miss during the St. Valentine's Day Massacre. *Courtesy of the* Chicago Daily News.

got out of a chauffeur-driven limousine in front of their house on Clyde Avenue, and Anna Torrio began to walk inside. As Torrio reached in to pick up some packages from their shopping trip, a black Cadillac screeched to a stop across the street. Inside, four men with pistols and shotguns watched for a moment, and then two of them, George "Bugs" Moran and Hymie Weiss, jumped from the car and ran toward Torrio with their guns blazing.

Torrio fell immediately with a bullet in his chest and one in his neck. Moran and Weiss ran to the fallen man and, standing above him, fired bullets into his right arm and another into his groin. Moran leaned over to put the next one into Torrio's head, but his gun was empty. As he reached for another clip, the driver began honking the horn of the Cadillac, signaling frantically that they needed to leave. Moran and Weiss ran to the car and they sped away.

Somehow, Torrio managed to crawl to the house, and his wife, who was screaming, came out and pulled him inside. A neighbor, who had witnessed the shooting, called an ambulance and Torrio was raced to the hospital. Unbelievably, he survived with a permanent scar to his neck. Reporters soon surrounded his hospital bed, demanding more information. Torrio stated that he knew all four of the assailants involved, but "I'll never tell their names," he said.

In February, Torrio (still bandaged) was sent to federal court for the brewery fiasco, and he received a nine-month jail sentence to be served in the Waukegan County jail, which had medical services for the ailing mobster. The treatment that Torrio received in prison was equal to the status of the gangland boss. The windows of his cell were covered with bulletproof glass, and extra deputies guarded him day and night. Easy chairs, throw rugs, books and other luxuries were added as well. Torrio also received the special privilege of taking his evening meals in the sheriff's home and being allowed to relax on the sheriff's front porch for awhile each night, visiting with his wife and associates like Al Capone.

As he finished serving his sentence, Torrio had a lot of time to think. When he got out, he announced that he was tired of the rackets and that he was turning his entire operation over to Capone. He just needed to get out of Chicago alive. Torrio and his wife left the city in an armor-plated limousine and were escorted by two roadsters filled with gunmen. When they reached a train station, just over the Indiana state line, Capone's men patrolled the station with machine guns until the train departed and took the Torrios to Florida. After that, they went on to Italy, where they lived in Naples for three years.

Torrio got bored in Italy, but knowing that he couldn't return to Chicago, he moved to New York instead and went into the real estate business with the blessing of Meyer Lansky and Charles "Lucky" Luciano. He also helped to establish a liquor cartel along the Atlantic seaboard and established himself as an elder statesman of the underworld. He lived a sedate and quiet life after Prohibition was repealed, but in 1936, he was arrested for income tax evasion. After a series of trials and appeals, he served two years in Leavenworth and was paroled in 1941. He died in a barber's chair (of natural causes) in 1957.

Torrio's departure from Chicago shoved Al Capone into the violent spotlight of the Chicago underworld, and it also made him the top man in the city at only twenty-five years of age. He now had an annual income that would actually land him a place in the *Guinness Book of World Records*. And he also had a bloody gang war on his hands.

On September 29, 1926, Capone was nearly killed when seventeen cars filled with North Side gangsters opened fire on the Hawthorne Hotel in Cicero, where he was having breakfast. They opened fire on the place, emptying clip after clip into the hotel, spraying everything in sight. Hymie Weiss boldly climbed from his car, with George Moran close behind him. Weiss ran up to the door of the hotel and opened fire with his machine gun, waving the weapon back and forth across the width of the passageway beyond the doors. When he finished firing, he walked coolly back to the car and they drove away. More than one thousand rounds had been fired into the building, and every window in the place was shattered. Amazingly, no one was killed.

On October 11, Capone retaliated. Hymie Weiss had just climbed out of his car outside of Holy Name Cathedral, heading toward his offices above O'Banion's old flower shop, when four men opened fire on him with machine guns. Another North Side gunman, Patrick Murray, died instantly on the street, but Weiss took ten bullets and survived long enough to be pronounced dead, without regaining consciousness, at the hospital. Meanwhile, the assassins disappeared into the crowds along Dearborn Street. A discarded machine gun was found in an alley off Dearborn, but it couldn't be traced back to the killers.

Soon, the other partners in the North Side gang were wiped out, or fled Chicago, one by one, leaving only George Moran.

George "Bugs" Moran was born in Minnesota in 1893 but moved to Chicago with his parents in 1900. He joined up with one of the North Side Irish gangs and was befriended by a young tough named Dion O'Banion. The two began working together, robbing warehouses, but after one fouled-up job, Moran was captured. He kept his silence and served two years in Joliet Prison without implicating O'Banion in the crime. He was released at age nineteen and went back to work with his friend. He was soon captured again and, once more, kept silent about those with whom he worked. He stayed in jail this time until 1923.

When Moran, known as "Bugs" because of his quick temper, got out of prison, he joined up with O'Banion's now formidable North Side mob. They had become a powerful organization, supplying liquor to Chicago's wealthy Gold Coast. Moran became a valuable asset, hijacking Capone's liquor trucks, and he was known as O'Banion's right-hand man, always impeccably dressed, right down to the two guns that he always wore. When O'Banion was killed in his flower shop in 1924, Moran swore revenge. The war that followed claimed many lives, and by 1927, Moran stood alone against the Capone mob, most of his allies having succumbed in the fighting.

In early 1929, Moran reportedly had one of Capone's gunmen, Pasquillano Lolordo, gunned down, and Capone vowed that he would have Moran wiped out on February 14. Capone was in Florida at the time, and he put in a call to Chicago. He had a very special "valentine" that he wanted delivered to Moran.

Through a contact, Capone arranged for someone to call Moran and tell him that a special shipment of hijacked whiskey was going to be delivered to one of Moran's garages on the North Side. Adam Heyer, a friend of Moran, owned the garage, and it was used as a distribution point for North Side liquor. A sign out front read "S-M-C Cartage Co. Shipping—Packing—Long Distance Hauling." It was located at 2122 North Clark Street.

On the morning of February 14, a group of Moran's men gathered at the Clark Street garage. One of the men was Johnny May, an ex-safecracker who had been hired by Moran as an auto mechanic. He was working on a truck that morning, with his dog, a German Shepherd named Highball, tied to the bumper. In addition, six other men waited for the truck of hijacked whiskey to arrive. The men were Frank and Pete Gusenberg; James Clark, Moran's brother-in-law; Adam Heyer; Al Weinshank; and Reinhardt Schwimmer, a young optometrist who had befriended Moran and hung around the liquor warehouse just for the thrill of rubbing shoulders with gangsters.

Moran was already late for the morning meeting. He was due to arrive at 10:30, but he didn't even leave for the rendezvous, in the company of Willie Marks and Ted Newberry, until several minutes after that. While the seven men waited inside the warehouse, they had no idea that a police car had pulled up outside, or that Moran had spotted the car as he was driving south on Clark Street and, rather than deal with what he believed was a shakedown, had stopped at the next corner for a cup of coffee.

The St. Valentine's Day Massacre

A crowd mills around outside of the S-M-C Cartage Co. on the day of the massacre. *Courtesy of the* Chicago Daily News.

Five men got out of the police car, two of them in uniforms and three in civilian clothing. They entered the building, and a few moments later, the clatter of machine gun fire broke the stillness of the snowy morning. Soon after, five figures emerged and drove away. May's dog, inside the warehouse, began barking and howling.

The landlady in the next building, Mrs. Jeanette Landesman, was bothered by the sound of the dog, and she sent one of her boarders, C.L. McAllister, to the garage to see what was going on. He came outside two minutes later, his face a pale white color. He ran frantically up the stairs to beg Mrs. Landesman to call the police. He cried that the garage was full of dead men!

The police were quickly summoned and, upon entering the garage, were stunned by the carnage. Moran's men had been lined up against the rear wall of the garage and sprayed with machine guns. Pete Gusenberg had died kneeling, slumped over a chair. James Clark had fallen on his face with half of his head blown away, and Heyer, Schwimmer, Weinshank and May were thrown lifeless onto their backs. Only one of the men survived the slaughter, and only for a few hours. Frank Gusenberg had crawled from the blood-

The St. Valentine's Day Massacre, February 14, 1929. *Courtesy of the* Chicago Daily News.

sprayed wall where he had fallen and ended up out in the middle of the dirty floor. He was rushed to the Alexian Brothers Hospital, barely hanging on. Police sergeant Clarence Sweeney leaned down close to him and asked who had shot him.

"No one—nobody shot me," he groaned, and he died later that night.

The death toll of the massacre stood at seven, but the killers had missed Moran. When the police contacted him later and asked who had sent the men to the garage, he "raved like a madman." To the newspapers, Moran targeted Capone as ordering the hit. He proclaimed, "Only Capone kills guys like that."

The St. Valentine's Day Massacre broke the power of the North Side gang and marked the end of any significant gang opposition to Capone. However, it was also the event that finally sparked the decline of Capone's criminal empire. He had just gone too far, and the authorities, and even Capone's adoring public, were ready to put an end to the bootleg wars. The massacre started a wave of reform that would put Capone out of power for good.

In May 1929, Capone was summoned to New York to meet with Meyer Lansky and Charles "Lucky" Luciano, who were in the process of forming a national crime syndicate. They were unhappy with the attention that Capone had attracted in Chicago and decided that it would be good public relations if Al Capone went to jail for a time. It was arranged for him to be arrested in Philadelphia on a charge of carrying a concealed weapon. Two detectives were paid $10,000 each to arrest him in the lobby of a movie theatre, charge him and get him sentenced as quickly as possible. It all happened in just sixteen hours, and Capone was sentenced to spend a term of one year at the Eastern State Penitentiary.

Capone continued to conduct business from prison. He was given a private cell and was allowed to make long-distance telephone calls from the warden's office and to meet with his lawyers and with Frank Nitti, Jake Guzik and his brother, Ralph, all of whom made frequent trips to Philadelphia. He was released two months early on good behavior, and when he returned to Chicago, he found himself branded public enemy number one.

When Capone returned to Chicago in March 1930, he found that the climate of the city had changed considerably during the time he had been away. His popularity had waned, and the police were adamant about putting his operations out of business. Police Captain John Stege even posted a guard of twenty-five policemen in front of the Capone home on Prairie Avenue with orders to arrest him as soon as he arrived from Pennsylvania. Capone slipped quietly into the city, though, and took up residence at the Hawthorne Inn in Cicero, where he spent four days answering mail and getting caught up on the state of operations. Then, he and his attorneys blatantly called on Captain Stege and the United States district attorney and found that neither of them had an actual warrant for his arrest. With that settled, he went home.

While no charges had actually been filed against Capone, there was nothing to prevent the police from keeping him under surveillance. Two uniformed policemen were assigned to follow Capone everywhere he went, day and night. Capone's empire was starting to crumble.

The United States government had now gotten involved in Chicago's dilemma over how to get rid of Capone. Washington dispatched a group of treasury agents (Eliot Ness and his "Untouchables") to harass Capone and try to find a way to bring down his operation. In the end, however, it would not be murder or illegal liquor that would get Capone—it would be income tax evasion. He was arrested on October 6, 1931, and indicted. On October 17, he was convicted on five counts, three of evading taxes from 1925 to 1928 and two of failing to file tax returns in 1928 and 1929. He was sentenced to spend eleven years in a federal prison. He was first sent to Atlanta and then, in 1934, was transferred to the brutal, "escape proof" prison known as Alcatraz.

The prison was a place of total punishment and few privileges. Many of the prisoners at Alcatraz went insane from the harsh conditions, and Capone was probably one of them. The beatings, attempts on his life and the prison routine took a terrible toll on Capone's mind. After he was nearly stabbed to death in the yard, he was excused from outdoor exercise and usually stayed inside and played a banjo that was given to him by his wife. He later joined the four-man prison band. After five years, though, Capone's mind snapped. He would often refuse to leave his cell and would sometimes crouch down in the corner and talk to himself. Another inmate recalled that on some days Capone would simply make and remake his bunk all day long. He spent the last portion of his stay in the prison hospital ward, being treated for an advanced case of syphilis. He left Alcatraz in 1939 and died in Florida in 1947.

The February 1929 massacre may have been the beginning of the end for Al Capone, but it also marked the decline of Bugs Moran. With the remnants of his gang, he attempted to take back control of the Gold Coast, but Capone's men were too powerful. His lot did improve somewhat after Capone went to prison in 1931, but it didn't last long.

The end of World War II reduced the once powerful gangster to petty burglaries. He first moved to downstate Illinois, St. Louis and then Ohio before a failed robbery got him arrested by the FBI. He was sentenced to serve ten years in prison in 1946, and his release found him quickly rearrested for another robbery. This time, he was sent to Leavenworth, where he died from lung cancer in February 1957.

It was a sad, and almost pathetic, ending for the gangster who was known after St. Valentine's Day 1929 as "the man who got away."

GIN AND JAZZ
AT THE GREEN MILL

Located on Chicago's North Side is one of the few reminders of the days of Al Capone that still exists: the legendary jazz club known as the Green Mill on North Broadway. As the city's oldest nightclub, it has been offering continuous entertainment since 1907 and remains today as an authentic link to not only Al Capone but also to the club's former manager and Capone henchman "Machine Gun" Jack McGurn.

The Green Mill opened in 1907 as Pop Morse's Roadhouse, and from the very beginning it was a favorite hangout for show business people in Chicago. In those days, actors from the North Side's Essanay Studios made the roadhouse a second home. One of the most popular stars to frequent the place was "Bronco Bill" Anderson, the star of dozens of silent Westerns from Essanay. Anderson often rode his horse to Pop Morse's, and the proprietor even installed a hitching post that Anderson's horse shared with those of other stars like Wallace Beery and William S. Hart. Back then, even screen greats like Charlie Chaplin stopped in occasionally for a drink.

Around 1910, the Chamales brothers purchased the club from the original owners. They installed a huge, green windmill on the roof and renamed the place the Green Mill Gardens. The choice of the name "Green Mill" was inspired by the infamous Moulin Rouge in Paris (*moulin rouge* is French for "red mill"), but green was chosen so that it would not be confused with any of the red-light districts in Chicago. The new owners added outdoor dancing and live entertainment in the enlarged sunken gardens and also added a rhumba room next door. Tom Chamales later went on to construct the Riviera Theatre, located around the corner from the Green Mill. He and his brother leased the Green Mill to Henry Van Horne, and it soon began to attract the best—and worst—of the late-night denizens of Chicago.

By the time that Prohibition arrived, the Green Mill had become known as the most jumping spot on the North Side. Jazz fans flocked to the club to savor this new and evolving musical art form, which had been born in the South but had been recreated in Chicago after World War I. The jazz crowd ignored the laws against alcohol and hid their bootleg whiskey in hip flasks, which they eagerly sipped at the Green Mill. The club helped to launch the careers of singers like Helen Morgan, Anita O'Day and Billie Holliday, all of whom went on to become legends. It also offered an endless procession of swinging jazz combos and vaudevillians who dropped in to jam or just to relax between sets at other clubs.

In the middle of the 1920s, Van Horne gave up his interest in the place, and the Chamales brothers leased the club to Al Capone's South Side mob. Capone himself, although straying into the enemy's territory on the North Side, often enjoyed hanging out at the club, listening to the music and drinking with friends. Capone had a trapdoor installed behind the bar that offered access to tunnels under the building, just in case the place was raided by the police or attacked by rival gangsters.

At the Green Mill, though, it's not the reminder of Al Capone that attracts crime buffs; it's the legend of Jack McGurn, who managed the club for Capone in the 1920s.

James Vincenzo De Mora, or Jack McGurn as he later became known, was born in Chicago's Little Italy in 1904. He grew up as a clean-cut kid from the slums who excelled in school and was an excellent boxer. A promoter managed to get him into the ranks of professional fighters, and at the man's suggestion James adopted the ring name of "Jack McGurn." He seemed to have a great career ahead, until his father, Angelo De Mora, a grocer with a store on Halsted Street, ran into trouble with the terrible Genna brothers.

At the start of Prohibition, the Gennas had transformed all of Little Italy into a vast commercial area of alcohol cookers. Stills were set up in almost every home, franchised by the Gennas, making homemade rotgut whiskey that was popular in neighborhood speakeasies. Angelo De Mora sold sugar to the Gennas for their operations, a relatively safe enterprise until some of his competitors shot Angelo to death in front of his store on January 8, 1923.

McGurn never got back into the ring. He was only nineteen years old, but he had a mother and siblings to take care of. He picked up a gun and started working for Al Capone, who regarded him as his most trustworthy gunman. He was given the most dangerous and grisly assignments, and within a few years, "Machine Gun" Jack McGurn was the most feared of Capone's killers.

McGurn relished his work, especially when six of his targets were part of the Genna mob, which he blamed for his father's death. In just over a

Gin and Jazz at the Green Mill

A vintage postcard of the Green Mill Gardens.

month's time, he wiped out all of the Gennas' top men. He learned that one of these men had referred to his father as a "nickel and dimer." So, after each of them had been machine-gunned to death, McGurn pressed a nickel into each of their palms, his sign of contempt and a trademark that would be forever linked to his murders.

McGurn continued to earn his pay and his fearsome reputation. Joe Aiello's feud with Capone over West Side beer territories reached its peak when Aiello offered a $50,000 reward for Capone's murder. He imported four out-of-town killers to do the job when no one in Chicago dared to cross Capone. Days after their arrival, the four men met the wrath of Jack McGurn. All of them were found riddled with machine-gun bullets—and with nickels pressed into their palms.

When not working for Capone, McGurn frequented Chicago's hottest jazz spots and managed to become part owner of several of them through intimidation and violence. By the time he was twenty-three, McGurn owned pieces of at least five nightclubs and managed a number of other lucrative properties. He also managed the Green Mill for Capone and was later given 25 percent of its ownership in exchange for his loyalty. This became his usual hangout, and he could often be found sipping liquor in one of the green-plush upholstered booths.

McGurn was fiercely loyal to the Green Mill, and in 1927, he became enraged when the club's star attraction, singer and comedian Joe E. Lewis,

The Green Mill today remains one of the hottest jazz clubs in the city.

refused to renew his contract, stating that he was going to work for a rival club. Lewis opened to a packed house at the New Rendezvous the next night. Days later, McGurn took Lewis aside as he was about to enter his hotel, the New Commonwealth. McGurn had two friends with him, and all three of them had their hands shoved in their pockets. McGurn told Lewis that they missed him at the club and that "the old Mill's a morgue without you." Lewis assured him that he would find another headliner, and when McGurn told him that he had made his point and needed to come back, Lewis refused. He bravely turned his back on the killer and walked away.

On November 27, three of McGurn's men stormed into Lewis's hotel suite, beat him and then cut his throat almost from ear to ear. The comedian survived the attack, managed to recover his singing voice and continued with his career. Capone, unhappy with McGurn's actions but unable to rebuke one of his best men, was said to have advanced Lewis $10,000 so that the performer could get back on his feet.

Gin and Jazz at the Green Mill

"Machine Gun" Jack McGurn's father was killed during the early beer wars in Chicago. After his father's death, McGurn went on to become Al Capone's right-hand man. He managed the Green Mill for Capone for several years. *Courtesy of the* Chicago Daily News.

A short time later, McGurn's own career was almost cut short. Two machine-gunners for George Moran, Pete and Frank Gusenberg (both killed during the St. Valentine's Day Massacre), caught up with McGurn in a phone booth inside the McCormick Inn. Several bursts from their Tommy guns almost finished McGurn for good, but major surgery, and a long period of secluded convalescence, saved the killer.

In early February 1929, McGurn visited Capone at his Palm Island, Florida home for a discussion about the North Side gang run by George Moran. Ten days later, the St. Valentine's Day Massacre took place.

McGurn has always been connected to the massacre, although that connection was never legally proven. A teenager named George Bricket was walking past the garage when five men entered on February 14. Bricket overheard one of the men call another "Mac"; he also picked out McGurn's photograph from police mug shots. Armed with an arrest warrant, police broke into McGurn's suite at the Stevens Hotel on February 27. As they hauled the gangster away, they were cussed out by McGurn's sweetheart, showgirl Louise Rolfe. The press dubbed her "the blonde alibi," and she swore that McGurn was with her at the time of the murders. McGurn was later indicted, but he married Louise soon after. Thanks to this, she was not required to testify against him.

McGurn's defense attorneys insisted four times that their client be brought to trial. Each time, the prosecution stated that it was not ready to proceed. Under Illinois law, the prosecution was only allowed four legal delays of this kind. After that, it had to drop the case. McGurn was set free on December 2, 1929.

McGurn's likely role in the St. Valentine's Day Massacre led to Capone putting him "on ice." He began to be seen less and less with the boss and was not seen at all during Capone's tax trial, when the job of bodyguard was given over to Phil D'Andrea.

Once Capone went to prison, McGurn's prestige started to slip. He busied himself with his nightclubs, most of which went under during the Depression, and Louise left him when his money ran out. Alone and flat broke; McGurn met his end on February 13, 1936, the eve of the anniversary of the St. Valentine's Day Massacre.

McGurn was in the middle of his third frame at the Avenue Recreation Parlor, a bowling alley located at 805 North Milwaukee Avenue, when remnants from the old Moran gang finally caught up with him. Five men burst into the bowling alley, and while three of them pretended to rob the place, the other two machine-gunned McGurn to death on the hardwood lanes.

Gin and Jazz at the Green Mill

In McGurn's left hand, the killers placed a comic valentine, which read:

> *You've lost your job.*
> *You've lost your dough,*
> *Your jewels and handsome houses.*
> *But things could be worse, you know.*
> *You haven't lost your trousers.*

In the palm of "Machine Gun" Jack McGurn's right hand, the killers placed a solitary nickel.

DEATH OF A
LABOR RACKETEER

THE ROGERS PARK KILLING OF "BIG TIM" MURPHY

Eighty years after the drive-by shooting that claimed the life of labor organizer and gangster "Big Tim" Murphy, the bullet holes from that violent summer night are still visible in the yellow brickwork of the common bungalow where he once lived. They serve as a visible reminder of a man who never achieved fame in the annals of Chicago crime but left a bloody mark on it nonetheless.

Timothy Murphy grew up in the "Back of the Yards" neighborhood on Chicago's South Side. He was a towering, slab-bodied and mostly genial boy who later boasted of selling newspapers to the famous meatpacker J. Ogden Armour outside of the main offices of Armour & Company at Forty-third and Racine. When he was older, Murphy got a job as a railroad switchman for the Chicago junction line, which would give him a lifelong sympathy for the plight of the working man.

Murphy was a devoted family man and had many friends. He was regarded as a great pal to just about everyone, but he had a dual nature that made him a dangerous man when provoked. All of the good work that he might have accomplished in labor organizing and politics was sabotaged by his associations with criminals and thugs—and by his own dabbling in crime. In 1909, he became involved with Mount Tennes, the so-called "Telegraph Gambling King" of Chicago. Tennes set up his first telegraph switchboard, located in a train station in Forest Park, and received race results from tracks in Illinois, Kentucky and New York. Tennes had an illegal monopoly on the information, and for a share of the profits, his operators sent the results to hundreds of bookie joints, gambling parlors and pool halls all over the city. Murphy's alliance with Tennes earned him a huge amount of money, but two years later, he sold Tennes out to a grand jury and walked away without a blemish on his record.

"Big Tim" Murphy and his wife, Florence, at a Chicago train station. *Courtesy of the* Chicago Daily News.

Death of a Labor Racketeer

While working with Tennes, Murphy had learned the art of bribing public officials and decided to try out politics. In 1915, he ran a highly successful campaign for the state legislature, getting elected from the working-class, Irish-Catholic Fourth Ward. He used the clever slogan of "Elect Big Tim Murphy—He's a Cousin of Mine!" Murphy spent just one term in Springfield, returned to Chicago and got involved in the labor rackets.

Through his friend Maurice "Mossie" Enright, an organizer with the American Federation of Labor and a convicted murderer, he was able to organize gas station attendants, garbage collectors and street sweepers. Strikes, wage increases and higher union dues followed, and Murphy got a percentage of everything. He and Enright operated from Old Quincy No. 9, a famous saloon at Randolph and LaSalle Streets, and for a time, the two men were inseparable. Eventually, they had a falling out over the division of proceeds from the settlement of a labor strike and their friendship came to an end. Like Mount Tennes years before, Enright was blindsided by Murphy's ruthless ambition.

On February 3, 1920, Enright was getting out of his car in front of his home on Garfield Boulevard when five men in another automobile pulled up and opened fire on him before he could draw his own revolver and defend himself. Enright was hit eleven times and was dead when the other car pulled away. His wife found him moments later, lying in a pool of his own blood. Tim Murphy, Michael Carozzo, the head of the Street Sweeper's Union and several others were arrested and questioned about the murder, but each man had an alibi and was let go. Enright's murder remains officially unsolved to this day.

Murphy continued to run the three unions but was too restless and greedy to be happy with the small amount of money that was coming in. In 1920, he organized his first mail robbery. It went off without a hitch, understated and bloodless, and took place after informants told Murphy about an overheard telephone conversation concerning money that was coming into the Pullman station. Two bags of cash that amounted to just over $125,000 were sent by insured, registered mail and arrived at the Illinois Central station in Pullman on August 30. When the train pulled in, a bank messenger named Minsch was waiting on the platform. He signed for the sacks and tossed them onto a mail chute. Three boys with a cart earned a quarter each from Minsch by loading whatever he sent down the chute into his car. The boys were waiting but had trouble lifting the two bags. Two men were standing nearby, apparently waiting for someone; they saw the boys and walked over to help. The boys directed the men to take the bags to Minsch's car, but they kept walking, tossed the two bags into the backseat of another car and drove away. One of the men was Big Tim Murphy and the other was his partner, Vincent Cosmano.

Unfortunately for Murphy, someone talked, and the two men were arrested and indicted by a grand jury. Murphy needed money for lawyers, so he decided to rob another train to get it. This time, he bribed a mail clerk in Indianapolis for a tip on a weekly shipment of cash and government Liberty Bonds that was sent to the Federal Reserve in Chicago. Murphy put together a crew (which included Cosmano, his longtime driver Ed Guerin, Mike Carozzo and two brothers, Frank and Pete Gusenberg) and they set up surveillance on the Dearborn Station at Polk Street. After they learned when the money shipment arrived, they pulled off the robbery on April 6. They escaped in a stolen Cadillac with $380,000.

It didn't take long for the police to get suspicious, and the mail clerk Murphy had bribed was the first to confess. Ed Guerin also talked because Murphy never gave him his share of the money. A judge issued a search warrant for the house where Murphy's father-in-law lived, and postal inspectors found a trunk in the attic that was so heavy with cash and bonds that it took four men to haul it out. The bills in the trunk were brand-new, and the Federal Reserve had a list of their serial numbers. The money, plus the two confessions, sent Murphy to Leavenworth for four years.

Murphy was washed up when he was released from prison, but an eternal optimist, he began devising new schemes to make money while his long-suffering wife, Florence, pestered him to find a suitable line of work. There was money to be made, and Murphy began devising a series of harebrained schemes that included a banana plantation in Texas, a portable grocery store on wheels, a dog track, a travel agency and even a plan to manufacture stop-and-go traffic lights. The latter was an idea ahead of its time, but no one was interested in what Big Tim was selling. He finally realized that it had been the union dues of the rank and file, not his get-rich-quick schemes, that made money, and he decided to take up where he had left off with labor organizing. He tried organizing tire dealers, jelly manufacturers, gasoline dealers and garage workers, but none of them worked out. Finally, he hatched a plan to take over the Cleaners and Dyers Union, a union with ten thousand members that was already controlled by Al Capone. Murphy stormed into the business office of the union on South Ashland Avenue with a gunman at his side and announced a "hostile takeover."

The union was interested, and Murphy's attempt to take over a union run by Capone was the last mistake that he ever made.

On the evening of June 28, 1928, Murphy was spending a quiet night at home in the West Rogers Park neighborhood on the far North Side. His wife

Death of a Labor Racketeer

State's attorney John E. Northrup looks over the infamous trunk that Murphy hid in his father-in-law's attic. It was so heavy with cash and bonds that it took four men to get it down the stairs. *Courtesy of the* Chicago Daily News.

was away at a church festival, and he was listening to the 1928 Democratic National Convention on the radio with his brothers-in-law, Harry and William Diggs. About 11:00 p.m., someone knocked loudly on the front door. Instead of going to the door, Murphy and Harry Diggs slipped out the side door and went around the house to see who was there. When they saw no one, Murphy walked across the front of the house and onto the lawn. Just then, gunfire broke out from a sedan that was parked on the street and Murphy was shot down in the yard. As the car sped away, the Diggs brothers spotted four men inside, although none of them was ever identified.

Murphy was carried into the house. As he lay dying, he tried desperately to say something to his brothers-in-law, but he died before he could speak. The

The West Rogers Park house where "Big Tim" Murphy was killed in June 1928. *Courtesy of the* Chicago Daily News.

police arrived before Florence returned from church. When she found her husband's bloody body lying on the living floor, she collapsed on top of him and began to weep. She promised revenge. According to the *Chicago Tribune*, she vowed, "If I knew who had killed Tim Murphy, I wouldn't tell anybody—I wouldn't wait for anybody. I'd take a gun and kill them as they killed him."

Big Tim Murphy was laid to rest at Holy Sepulchre Cemetery, and unlike the gaudy gangster funerals of the 1920s, only a modest crowd attended the service. There were no gangland officials or politicians at the service, although a few South Side and "Back of the Yards" personages did turn out for the wake the night before the burial. Too much had changed while Murphy had been in prison, and his hold on the Chicago rackets had slipped away in his absence. He was not a man anyone wanted to get close to, and even the tags on the funeral flowers were removed so that no outsider had the opportunity to know who sent them. The church refused every form of funeral service, and an old friend who was an undertaker on the South Side recited the Lord's Prayer, the only words spoken over his body.

It was a sad end to a man who started out with a lot of potential. In the end, it was greed and a failure to realize when ambition had gone too far that finally cost him his life.

THE LUETGERT
SAUSAGE VAT MURDER

The Adolph Luetgert murder case is one of the most gruesome in Chicago history. The story of the North Side sausage maker who decided to get rid of his troublesome wife is more chilling than almost any other crime. The murder sent a thrill of horror through the city as newspapers readers tried to imagine the harrowing murder scene and the dark basement where the evidence nearly disappeared. Thanks to the vivid imagination of the average reader, the Luetgert case earned an unusual spot in the annals of Chicago crime as the only murder to ever drastically affect the sale of food.

Adolph Luetgert was born in Germany and came to America after the Civil War. In 1872 he arrived in Chicago, where he pursued several trades, including farming and leather tanning, and eventually started a wholesale liquor business near Dominick Street. He later turned to sausage making, the field in which he found his greatest success. After discovering that his German-style sausages were quite popular in Chicago, he built a sausage plant in 1894 at the southwest corner of Hermitage and Diversey. Here the massive German would achieve his greatest success—and his continued infamy.

Although the hardworking Luetgert soon began to put together a considerable fortune, he was an unhappy and restless man. Luetgert had married his first wife, Caroline Rabaker, in 1872. She gave birth to two boys, only one of whom survived childhood. Caroline died five years later, in November 1877. Luetgert sold his liquor business in 1879 and moved to North and Clybourn Avenues, where he started his first sausage-packing plant in the same building he used as a residence. Two months after Caroline's death, Luetgert remarried an attractive, younger woman. This did little to ease his restlessness, however, and he was rumored to be engaged in several affairs during the time when he built a three-story frame

Adolph Luetgert in 1898. *Courtesy of the* Chicago Tribune.

house next door to the sausage factory. He resided there with his son and new wife.

His wife, Louisa Bicknese Luetgert, was a beautiful woman who was ten years younger than her husband. She was a former servant from the Fox River Valley who met her new husband by chance. He was immediately taken with her, entranced by her diminutive stature and tiny frame. She was less than five feet tall and looked almost childlike next to her burly husband. As a wedding gift, he gave her a unique, heavy gold ring with her initials inscribed inside it. He had no idea at the time that this ring would later be his undoing.

After less than three years of business, Luetgert's finances began to fail. Even though his factory turned out large quantities of sausages, Luetgert found that he could not meet his supplier's costs. Instead of trying to reorganize his finances, however, he and his business advisor, William Charles, made plans to expand. They attempted to secure more capital to enlarge the factory, but by April 1897 it had all fallen apart. Luetgert, deep in depression, sought solace with his various mistresses, and his excesses, as well as his business losses, began taking a terrible toll on his marriage. Neighbors frequently heard him and Louisa arguing, and their disagreements became so heated that Luetgert eventually moved his bedroom from the house to a small chamber inside the factory. Soon after, Louisa found out that her husband was having an affair with the family's maid, Mary Simerling, who also happened to be Louisa's niece. She was enraged at this news, and this new scandal attracted the attention of the people in the neighborhood who were already gossiping about the couple's marital woes.

Luetgert soon gave the neighbors even more to gossip about. One night, during another shouting match with Louisa, he responded to her indignation over his affair with Mary by taking his wife by the throat and choking her. Before she collapsed, Luetgert saw neighbors peering in at him from the parlor window of their home, and he released her. A few days later, Luetgert was seen chasing his wife down the street, shouting and waving a revolver. After a couple of blocks, Luetgert broke off the chase and walked silently back to the factory.

Then, on May 1, 1897, Louisa disappeared. When questioned about it, Luetgert stated that Louisa had gone out the previous evening to visit her sister. After several days, though, she did not come back. Soon after, Diedrich Bicknese, Louisa's brother, came to Chicago and called on his sister. He was informed that she was not at home. He came back later and, finding Luetgert at home, demanded to know where Louisa was. Luetgert calmly told him that Louisa had disappeared on May 1 and had never returned.

When Diedrich demanded to know why Luetgert had not informed the police about Louisa's disappearance, the sausage maker simply told him that he was trying to avoid a scandal but that he had paid two detectives five dollars to try and find her.

Diedrich immediately began searching for his sister. He went to Kankakee, thinking that perhaps she might be visiting friends there, but found no one who had seen her. He returned to Chicago, and when he found that Louisa still had not come home, now having abandoned her children for days, he went to the police and spoke with Captain Herman Schuettler.

The detective and his men began to search for Louisa. They questioned neighbors and relatives and heard many recitations about the couple's violent arguments. Captain Schuettler was familiar with Luetgert and had had dealings with him in the past. He summoned the sausage maker to the precinct house on two occasions and each time pressed him about his wife. Schuettler recalled a time when the Luetgerts had lost a family dog, an event that prompted several calls from Luetgert, but when his wife had gone missing, he noted that Luetgert had never contacted him. Luetgert again used the excuse that as a prominent businessman, he could not afford the disgrace and scandal.

The police began searching the alleyways and dragging the rivers, but they also went to the sausage factory and began questioning the employees. One of them, Wilhelm Fulpeck, recalled seeing Louisa around the factory at about 10:30 p.m. on May 1. A young German girl named Emma Schiemicke had passed by the factory with her sister at about the same time on that evening and remembered seeing Luetgert leading his wife up the alleyway behind the factory.

Frank Bialk, a night watchman at the plant, confirmed both stories. He had also seen Luetgert and Louisa at the plant that night. He only got a glimpse of Louisa but had seen his employer several times. Shortly after the couple entered the factory, Luetgert had come back outside and had given Bialk a dollar and asked him to get him a bottle of celery compound from a nearby drugstore. When the watchman returned with the medicine, he was surprised to find that the door leading into the main factory was locked. Luetgert appeared and took the medicine. He made no comment about the locked door and sent Bialk back to the engine room.

A little while later, Luetgert again approached the watchman and sent him back to the drugstore to buy a bottle of medicinal spring water. While the watchman had been away running errands, Luetgert had apparently been working alone in the factory basement. He had turned on the steam under the middle vat at a little before 9:00 p.m., and it was still running when Bialk returned. The watchman reported that Luetgert had remained in the basement until about 2:00 a.m.

Bialk found Luetgert fully dressed in his office the next day. He asked whether or not the fires under the vat should be put out, and Luetgert told him to leave them burning, which was odd since the factory had been closed for several weeks during Luetgert's financial reorganization. Bialk did as he was told, however, and went down to the basement. Here, he saw a hose sending water into the middle vat, and on the floor in front of it was a sticky, glue-like substance. Bialk noticed that it seemed to contain bits of bone, but he thought nothing of it. Luetgert used all sorts of waste meats to make his sausage and he assumed that this was all it was.

On May 3, another employee, Frank Odorowsky, known as "Smokehouse Frank," also noticed the slimy substance on the factory floor. He feared that someone had boiled something in the factory without Luetgert's knowledge, so he went to his employer to report it. Luetgert told him not to mention the brown slime. As long as he kept silent, Luetgert said, he would have a good job for the rest of his life. Frank went to work scraping the slime off the floor and poured it into a nearby drain that led to the sewer. The larger chunks of waste were placed in a barrel, and Luetgert told him to take the barrel out to the railroad tracks and scatter the contents there.

Following these interviews, Schuettler made another disturbing and suspicious discovery. A short time before Louisa's disappearance, even though the factory had been closed during the reorganization, Luetgert had ordered 325 pounds of crude potash and 50 pounds of arsenic from Lor Owen & Company, a wholesale drug firm. It was delivered to the factory the next day. Another interview with Frank Odorowsky revealed what had happened to the chemicals. On April 24, Luetgert had asked Smokehouse Frank to move the barrel of potash to the factory basement, where there were three huge vats that were used to boil down sausage material. The corrosive chemicals were all dumped into the middle vat, and Luetgert turned on the steam beneath it, dissolving the material into liquid.

Combining this information with the eyewitness accounts, Captain Schuettler began to theorize about the crime. Circumstantial evidence seemed to show that Luetgert had killed his wife and boiled her in the sausage vats to dispose of the body. The more that the policeman considered this, the more convinced he became that this was what had happened. Hoping to prove his theory, he and his men started another search of the sausage factory, and he soon made a discovery that became one of the most gruesome in the history of Chicago crime.

On May 15, a search was conducted of the twelve-foot-long, five-foot-deep middle vat, two-thirds of which was filled with a brownish, brackish liquid. The officers drained the greasy paste from the vat, using gunnysacks as filters, and began poking through the residue with sticks. Here, Officer Walter Dean found several pieces of bone and two gold rings. One of them was a badly tarnished friendship ring and the other was a heavy gold band that had been engraved with the initials "L.L."

Louisa Luetgert had worn both of the rings.

After they were analyzed, the bones were found to be definitely human: a third rib; part of a humerus, or great bone, in the arm; a bone from the palm of a human hand; a bone from the fourth toe of a right foot; fragments of bone from a human ear; and a larger bone from a foot.

Adolph Luetgert, proclaiming his innocence, was arrested for the murder of his wife shortly after the search. Louisa's body was never found, and there were no witnesses to the crime, but police officers and prosecutors believed the evidence was overwhelming. Luetgert was indicted for the crime a month later, and details of the murder shocked the city's residents, especially those on the North Side. Even though Luetgert was charged with boiling his wife's body, local rumor had it that she had been ground into sausage instead! Needless to say, sausage sales declined substantially in 1897.

Luetgert's first trial ended with a hung jury on October 21 after the jurors failed to agree on a suitable punishment. Some argued for the death penalty, while others voted for life in prison. Only one of the jurors thought that Luetgert might be innocent. A second trial was held, and on February 9, 1898, Luetgert was convicted and sentenced to a life term at Joliet Prison. He was taken away, still maintaining his innocence and claiming that he would receive another trial. He was placed in charge of meats in the prison's cold-storage warehouse, and officials described him as a model inmate.

By 1899, though, Luetgert began to speak less and less and often quarreled with the other convicts. He soon became a shadow of his former, blustering persona, fighting for no reason and often babbling incoherently in his cell at night. His mind had been broken, either from guilt over his heinous crime or from the brutal conditions of the penitentiary. Luetgert died in 1900, likely from heart trouble. According to the *Chicago Daily Tribune*, the coroner who conducted the autopsy reported that his liver was greatly enlarged and in such a condition of degeneration that "mental strain would have caused his death at any time."

The sausage factory stood empty for years, looming over the neighborhood as a grim reminder of the horrors that had visited there. The windows of the place became a target for rocks thrown from the nearby railroad embankment, and the site often invited forays by the curious and the homeless.

In the months that followed his death, Luetgert's business affairs were entangled in litigation. The courts finally sorted everything out in August 1900, and a public auction was held for the factory and its grounds. Portions of the property were divided between several buyers, but the Library Bureau Company, which was founded by Dewey Decimal System creator Melvil Dewey, leased the factory itself. The company used it as a workshop and storehouse for its line of library furniture and office supplies. During the renovations, the infamous vats in the basement were discarded.

In June 1904, a devastating fire swept through the old sausage factory. It took more than three hours to put out the blaze, and when it was over, the building was still standing but everything inside had been destroyed.

Despite the damage done to the building's interior, the Library Bureau reopened its facilities in the former sausage factory. It would go on to change owners many times in the decades that followed. In 1907, a contracting

The Luetgert Sausage Factory at Hermitage and Diversey. *Courtesy of the* Chicago Tribune.

mason purchased the old Luetgert house and moved it from behind the factory to another lot in the neighborhood, hoping to dispel the grim memories attached to it. The part of Hermitage Avenue that intersected with Diversey was closed. By the 1990s, the factory stood empty and crumbling, facing a collection of empty lots that were only interrupted by the occasional ramshackle frame house.

In 1999, around the 100th anniversary of the death of Adolph Luetgert, the former sausage factory was converted into loft condominiums, and a brand-new neighborhood sprang up to replace the aging homes that remained from the days of the Luetgerts. Fashionable brick homes and apartments appeared around the old factory, and rundown taverns were replaced with coffee shops.

The old neighborhood was gone, but the stories of this infamous crime still lingered, providing the area with a unique place in history as the site of the only Chicago murder that ever discouraged people from eating sausages!

THE LINCOLN AVENUE
STREETCAR MURDER

O ne of the most tragic murders to occur on Chicago's North Side took place at a former streetcar stop at Carmen and Lincoln Avenues. It was at this corner on November 18, 1905, that the life of young Lizzie Kaussehull was cut short by a crazed stalker, Edward Rodhaubt, who had been pursuing her for three months.

During that time, Rodhaubt had tried unsuccessfully to win Lizzie's heart. He constantly bothered her, wrote her letters, sent her flowers and simply refused to accept her rejection. Neighbors later recalled that he frequently waited around the corner of Lincoln and Carmen, watching for the streetcar that would bring Lizzie home from her job at Moeller & Stange's grocery store, located farther south on Lincoln. No one knew where the young man lived, but it was thought to be somewhere in the neighborhood, where he worked as a laborer. Each day, he waited for Lizzie as she stepped off the streetcar. She tried her best to ignore him, but Rodhaubt always followed the nineteen-year-old all the way to her front door at number 15 Carmen (now 2414 West Carmen). A reporter for the *Chicago Daily Tribune* later noted that neighbors claimed that Robhaut looked "demented."

Lizzie became so fearful for her life that her family reported Rodhaubt's behavior to the police, including the fact that he told Lizzie that he would kill her if she would not marry him. Rodhaubt was arrested, and a restraining order (called a "peace bond" in those days) was filed against him on November 11. It had no effect. He continued to follow her home from the streetcar stop each afternoon, begging her to marry him and threatening to kill her if she did not. Needless to say, Lizzie was terrified, but she was so intimidated by Rodhaubt that she feared calling the police again. For this reason, she said nothing to her family or the authorities. After a few days, Rodhaubt vanished, and Lizzie began to believe that he was finally going to leave her alone.

A Chicago streetcar on Lincoln Avenue. *Courtesy of the* Chicago Daily News.

The Lincoln Avenue Streetcar Murder

On November 18, Lizzie finished her shift at Moeller & Stange's and, as always, rode the streetcar north on Lincoln. When she reached her stop, she stepped off with several girlfriends, all of them laughing and talking. Then, suddenly, she saw Rodhaubt leaning against the wall of a nearby storefront. Lizzie's friends froze, and Lizzie shakily put up a hand and stammered in his direction that the peace bond was still in place against him. Her words had no more effect against Robhaut than the legal papers did—he ran toward her, and Lizzie began to scream.

Rodhaubt sprang on her and plunged a knife into Lizzie's chest. She staggered back away from him, but he attacked again, stabbing her three more times. Finally, her dress soaked with blood, she fell to the sidewalk. Rodhaubt looked down at the woman he claimed to love so much that he had to kill her because he couldn't have her, drew a revolver, placed the barrel into his mouth and pulled the trigger. The back of Rodhaubt's skull blew out in a red spray of gore, and his body collapsed on top of Lizzie's.

They were finally together—in death.

THE CASE OF THE "RAGGED STRANGER"

There has likely been no other murder case in the country that was as colorfully solved as the Chicago case of the "Ragged Stranger." It has been recounted many times over the years; in books, in detective magazines and even in a Hollywood movie. There have been a number of different writers who have taken credit for solving the case, and it's likely that this was one time when the press and the police department pooled their resources and brought a killer, a former war hero named Carl Wanderer, to justice.

Carl Otto Wanderer was born and raised in Chicago. His parents, German immigrants, taught him the value of a dollar at a young age, and by the time he was twenty-seven, he had saved enough to open a successful butcher shop with his father. His strict upbringing and frugal ways left Wanderer an unhappy and restless young man, and in 1916, adventure began to call to him.

The newspapers recounted the raids by Pancho Villa into the southwestern United States and called for volunteers to help pursue the Mexican bandit and his men. Wanderer enlisted in the military and was sent to New Mexico to serve under Black Jack Pershing as a cavalry officer. His experience with the First Illinois Cavalry gave him enough military stature to earn him a promotion to lieutenant with the first units sent to France when the United States entered World War I. He saw action on the Western Front and returned home, with medals for bravery, in the spring of 1919.

On October 1 of that same year, Wanderer married his sweetheart, a chubby but attractive twenty-year-old named Ruth Johnson. The couple moved into an apartment shared by Ruth's parents, and it was there that any affection that he had for her died. The claustrophobic flat became unbearable, thanks to Ruth's neediness and his nagging mother-in-law, who berated Wanderer about the fact that he didn't have enough money for the

Carl Wanderer. *Courtesy of the* Chicago Daily News.

couple to get a place of their own. Carl's restlessness once more got the better of him, and he began dating a sixteen-year-old typist named Julia Schmitt. He often met her at the Riverview Amusement Park while his wife was otherwise engaged.

And then, shortly before Christmas, Ruth happily announced to her husband that she was pregnant. Carl accepted the news with dismay and fell into somber, sullen moods. He rarely spoke and avoided coming home. He pondered his options and, as it turned out, bided his time, until a plan to rid himself of his problems slowly came to mind.

On June 21, 1920, Ruth and Carl attended an evening performance of a movie called *The Sea Wolf*, a rousing Jack London adventure story, at the Pershing Theatre (now the Davis) at Lincoln and Western. As they strolled home afterward, Wanderer later reported seeing a sinister-looking man lurking near Zindt's Drug Store on Lawrence Avenue. According to his story, the man crushed out a cigarette as they passed by and then followed behind them at a distance.

"Ruth went up ahead of me when we reached the house. She opened the outer door and I heard her fumbling with her keys to the inner door of the hall," Wanderer later told the police. Ruth reached up for the ribbon dangling from the overhead light so that she could find the right key. Carl asked her if she was having trouble and she laughed. Neither of them noticed the man who followed them into the dark vestibule. The "Ragged Stranger," as this man would come to be known, stepped forward with a gun trained on Ruth. "Don't turn on the light," the man said "Throw up your hands!"

Before Ruth and Carl could comply with his order, the stranger fired two bullets into Ruth. Wanderer claimed that he heard the man shout out a string of obscenities as he continued to fire. Carl jerked out his own Colt .45 service weapon and emptied it in the direction of the dark figure. It was later discovered that fourteen bullets had been fired in the small vestibule in a matter of a few seconds. When the smoke cleared, the stranger—and Ruth Wanderer—was lying on the floor of the vestibule, sprawled out in a widening pool of blood.

Ruth's mother rushed down to the door to find that her daughter had fallen with two bullets lodged in her. Wanderer had gone berserk with rage, smashing his gun and his fists against a man who was lying on the floor. Ruth lived just long enough to utter a few tragic words: "My baby...My baby is dead."

Detective Sergeant John Norton arrived on the scene just minutes later. By this time, neighbors and onlookers had started to gather around Wanderer, who was covered in the stranger's blood. Ruth's mother was cradling her daughter's lifeless body in her arms. Norton pushed his way through the crowd. The hulking detective was well known in the neighborhood, having been shot four times during his celebrated career, and everyone knew that he would get answers quickly in the case. He started off with just one question: why was Carl Wanderer carrying a gun?

Wanderer had a quick answer: there had been a robbery attempt at his father's butcher shop a short time before, and Carl was carrying his service revolver in case it happened again. He suggested to Norton that perhaps this man could have been involved. A search of the stranger's body turned up just $3.80 and a business card from a traveling circus. There was nothing else on the body, which was taken to Ravenswood Hospital for a check of fingerprints and an inquest. During questioning, Carl decided to embellish his connections with the stranger a little further. He looked familiar to him, Wanderer said. He believed the man had flirted with Ruth a few nights earlier. She had come home and reported the news to Carl in a near panic, terrified that "the stranger was laying a trap."

The morning editions of the Chicago newspapers jumped all over the story. They told of Wanderer's heroics and exemplary military record, touting his service in New Mexico and in Europe. He was a Great War hero who had fought to protect America from its enemies, they said, and now this same man had been forced to endure the coldblooded murder of his wife and unborn child. It was a heartless and horrible crime, and the public reacted with shock and outrage.

Carl Wanderer was awarded the status of a hero who had defended the honor of his wife, even though the end result had been tragic. The public expected to see him charged with nothing more than justifiable homicide in the murder of the "Ragged Stranger." He deserved to be left alone to grieve for his family, they believed, and this should be the end of the story.

But little did they know—the story of the "Ragged Stranger" was just getting started.

Detective John Norton, along with help from legendary crime reporter Harry Romanoff and his editor at the *Chicago Herald-Examiner*, Walter Howey, began to ask some hard questions about Wanderer's version of the murders.

To start with, there was the matter of the two guns that had been used. Both of them were big, .45-caliber automatics. Carl Wanderer's gun was explained in that it was his service pistol, but what about the matching weapon owned by the stranger? Howey and Norton could not understand how the man could have afforded such an expensive sidearm. A man who was down on his luck could have easily hocked the weapon and made a decent amount of money. This should have been preferable to risking a street robbery. It didn't make sense, so Romanoff sent a telegram to the Colt firearms company that contained the serial number of the stranger's gun. A reply soon came back. The gun had first been sold in 1913 to Von Lengerke & Antoine Sporting Goods Store in Chicago. The reporter checked with the store and found that Peter Hoffman, a telephone repairman who lived on Crawford Avenue, had purchased the gun.

The next day, Romanoff went to see Hoffman and discovered that he had sold the gun to his brother-in-law several years before. The brother-in-law's name was Fred Wanderer, Carl's cousin. Stunned, the reporter confronted Fred Wanderer with the information about where his gun had ended up. Fred admitted that he had gotten a gun from Peter Hoffman, but he had loaned it to his cousin, Carl, on June 21 and didn't have it anymore. Suddenly, Fred realized that this had been the day when Ruth had been killed. When this occurred to him, he was so shocked that he fainted.

Romanoff reported the problems with the gun to Detective Norton and Summerdale police lieutenant Mike Loftus. Carl Wanderer was brought in for questioning and was confronted with what had been discovered about the gun. Wanderer shrugged it off. He admitted that he had been carrying Fred's gun, and apparently the other one, which had been used by the "Ragged Stranger," was mistakenly identified as his. As it turned out, this was a possibility. A check with the Colt Company revealed that the other gun had been part of a massive shipment of weapons sent to military training camps during the war. The whole thing, Carl assured them, was all an innocent mistake.

Loftus and Romanoff were not convinced. While Carl was delayed at the police station, the two men went to Wanderer's house to speak with Ruth's mother. While Loftus engaged the woman in conversation, Romanoff searched Wanderer's bedroom and found incriminating photos of Carl and portions of love letters that had been written to Julia Schmitt, the young woman he had been seeing without Ruth's knowledge. When Julia was tracked down, she unraveled Carl's story, and the motive for the murder became clear. Carl Wanderer had wanted to get rid of his wife and arranged to have someone carry out the crime.

When confronted with this new information, Wanderer finally confessed. Carl had grown to hate his wife, he told detectives, and longed to be free of her so that he could marry Julia. Knowing that he could not commit the murder himself, he began hanging around seedy saloons until he met Al Watson (whose real name may have been Bernard T. Ryan), a Canadian ex-soldier who was living in a flophouse on Madison Street, Chicago's skid row. Wanderer told Watson that he was trying to win back his wife's affections and wanted to seem like a hero to her. He would pay him five dollars down and five dollars upon completion to carry out a phony robbery. Carl would hand Watson a gun when the couple went into the dark vestibule, and then he would slug Carl with it. Wanderer would seem to fight the man off, and Watson would run away, restoring Ruth's faith in his hero status.

Watson saw it as a harmless way to make a few bucks, and so he agreed. When Watson came into the vestibule that night, however, Carl did not hand him a gun. Instead, he cocked both weapons and fired at both Ruth and Watson at the same time. After they had fallen, he fired several more shots to make sure they were dead and then went into his "avenging husband act" for Ruth's mother, whom he knew would rush to the scene.

Carl Wanderer was twice indicted and twice convicted, once for the murder of Ruth Johnson Wanderer and once for the death of Al Watson. After his first trial, Wanderer was sentenced to serve twenty years, which so outraged editor Walter Howey that he used the editorial might of his widely read newspaper to keep the story alive and to demand a new trial. Public outrage resulted in a second trial and a death sentence for Wanderer.

While Carl was in jail, awaiting the hangman, he became a favorite subject for doctors, who tried to discover whether he had been insane when he planned his wife's death, and for reporters, who kept milking a good story. Some of Wanderer's favorite visitors were Ben Hecht and Charley MacArthur, two of the most famous writers from Chicago journalism's most colorful and sensational era. They were covering Carl's story for their respective newspapers and visited him often, playing poker with him and becoming quite chummy. They even convinced Carl to read two letters that they had written, hilariously attacking their bosses, from the gallows. The newsmen didn't remember until the last minute that Carl's hands and feet would be bound when he was executed so he couldn't read the letters. They asked him to croon a rendition of the maudlin tune "Old Pal, Why Don't You Answer Me?" moments before the drop instead.

On the day of his hanging, Carl was brought to the gallows, and to the surprise of everyone, save for Hecht and MacArthur, Wanderer began to sing. The hangman came forward after the first chorus, but Wanderer warned him away with a shake of his head. After the second chorus, even though Carl was still singing, the black shroud was placed over his head. When the song finally finished, he was asked if he had anything to say. "Christ have mercy on my…" Carl Wanderer began but never finished his plea. The trap sprung open and Carl shot downwards until the rope snapped tight and instantly killed him.

Charley MacArthur had the last word. He turned to his friend Ben Hecht and said with a sigh, "You know, Ben, that son-of-a-bitch would have been a hell of a song plugger."

THE "GIRL BANDIT"

News of a "girl bandit" made sensational headlines in the *Chicago Daily Tribune* after the murder of eighteen-year-old Edward Lehman on November 4, 1923. Lehman was killed during a robbery attempt at the Delson Knitting Works, located on Lincoln Avenue on the city's North Side. Lehman and night watchman Al Stemwedel discovered the thieves forcing their way into the building at 4:50 a.m., and both men were shot by the thieves, believed to be a man and a woman. Lehman later died at the nearby Alexian Brothers Hospital after gasping out a final statement, "Get Bockelman—he shot me."

Soon after, police arrested Walter Bockelman, twenty-five, who was familiar to both Lehman and Stemwedel. Lehman had also accused Bockelman of taking part in another robbery at a garage at 5833 Winthrop. The owner, Richard C. Tesmer, had been killed during the robbery, and a man and woman were seen fleeing the scene. Reports later claimed that night watchman Stemwedel knew Bockelman because the two of them had developed "bad blood" over a girl. After Lehman's dying statement, Bockelman and his alleged girlfriend, Ethel Beck, were brought in for questioning.

Ethel was picked up at the Drummond Athletic Club, "an alleged disorderly resort at Southport and Lill avenues"; in other words, a brothel. Newspapers reported that the nineteen-year-old waitress had six aliases, an unknown Greek husband and three arrests for prostitution. After being brought in, she confessed to taking part in the robbery that had led to the death of Edward Lehman. One witness, the *Chicago Daily Tribune* colorfully noted, described the getaway car as "driving rapidly west on Barry and north on Lincoln Avenue, a slim ankle of the girl hanging over the running board of the car."

Reporters loved printing everything they could about the "bandit queen." They went into detail about her impoverished and promiscuous life, her childhood abuse and her description of "stringy blond hair, the sleazy silk dress of faded red, the imitation fur coat, the poor teeth, and the rundown slippers." It was said that after Ethel's parents died, her two brothers were put into boarding schools, her sisters were sent to live with a family and she moved in with another family, who put her to work in a factory. After that, she became a waitress. In the *Daily Tribune*, Ethel was quoted as saying, "That's what I really like and if I got out of this mess, yes, man, I'd like to have a restaurant of my own. I made $18 a week and tips, as a waitress. But a girl's always getting into trouble, workin' around. Once I worked in a chop suey joint; not so good." The reporter pointed out that if Ethel was unable to open her own restaurant, she planned to star in the movies, where they wear lovely clothes.

Bockelman had another story altogether. He claimed that not only was he not involved in the robbery (Lehman had set him up, he said) but also that he had never met Ethel Beck. According to the *Daily Tribune*, he told police and reporters, "I never met her. I have an alibi, and when I get a lawyer I'll give a statement of where I was. But that girl, I never met her in my life."

Bockelman's wife was also talking to reporters, telling yet another story. She told the press that Walter had been a model husband until just a year before, when he start abusing her and their children. She stated that she hoped he and Ethel Beck would be hanged for Lehman's murder.

The sensationalistic case took another strange turn a short time later when another man, Otto Malm, came forward and confessed to the Lehman murder. He also implicated his common-law wife, Katherine, in the robbery and named Eric Noren as the man who drove the getaway car. The pair received life sentences for the murder, and Noren got off with fourteen years at Joliet Penitentiary.

As for Ethel Beck, she recanted her story and admitted that she had never been out with Bockelman. Being accused of robbery and murder just seemed like a good way to get some attention.

DILLINGER—DEAD OR ALIVE!

O n the evening of July 22, 1934, a dapper-looking man wearing a straw hat and a pinstriped suit stepped out of the Biograph Theatre on Lincoln Avenue on Chicago's North Side. He and two female friends had gone to see a film called *Manhattan Melodrama* starring Clark Gable. But no sooner had the trio reached the sidewalk than a man appeared and identified himself as Melvin Purvis of the FBI. Purvis ordered the man in the straw hat to surrender, but he decided to run instead. Several shots rang out, and the fleeing man fell dead to the pavement, his left eye shredded by shots fired by the other agents who lay in wait.

It only took a few bullets to end the life of John Herbert Dillinger, the most prolific bank robber in modern American history and the general public's favorite public enemy number one.

Dillinger was born in Indianapolis, Indiana, in 1903 and was, by all accounts, a quiet child with good grades who was popular with friends and teachers. When he was quite young, he proved to be an excellent athlete, especially excelling at baseball. He did have a minor brush with the law in the sixth grade, when he stole coal from the Pennsylvania Railroad yards and sold it to his neighbors.

After a short stint in the navy, he deserted and made his way back to Indiana. In September 1924, Dillinger finally stepped completely over the line of the law when he and a friend botched the robbery of a grocery store owner. Dillinger was caught and received a lengthy sentence at the Indiana State Reformatory. In jail, he befriended some bank robbers, who honed his skills, and when he was freed in May 1933, he began robbing small banks all over the state. With the resulting take, he arranged a prison break for his friends who were still behind bars.

Dillinger began making a name for himself as a dapper, polite bank robber with a sense of fair play. He only took money that belonged to the bank, and

John Dillinger, America's favorite public enemy. *Courtesy of the Library of Congress.*

his dashing good looks and flashy getaway cars earned him plenty of space in newspaper columns. The gang made their home base in Chicago, living in twos and threes in several apartments on Chicago's North Side. None of them drank hard liquor, sticking only to an occasional beer, so as not to draw any unwanted attention. They continued to rob banks, and after a robbery in Milwaukee, they decided to winter in Florida and Tucson, Arizona. During this time, two unknown men robbed a bank in East Chicago, Indiana, and Dillinger and gang member John Hamilton were accused of the crime. Dillinger was also said to have killed a police officer during the robbery, something that he always denied.

In Tucson, the gang was identified and arrested, and Dillinger was extradited to Indiana to stand trial for the East Chicago robbery—the one robbery that he probably didn't commit. Dillinger was locked up at the "escape proof" Lake County Jail in Crown Point, which held him for just one month. On March 3, 1934, Dillinger escaped using a fake gun that he

Dillinger—Dead or Alive!

The Biograph Theatre on Lincoln Avenue in the 1930s. *Courtesy of the* Chicago Tribune.

had carved and blackened with shoe polish. In minutes, he rounded up a dozen guards and made his way down a flight of stairs with a couple of the officers as hostages. He drove along back roads until he made it into rural Illinois. He let the officers out along the side of the road and gave them four dollars for food and carfare. Dillinger apologized and told them that he would have given them more if he had it.

Dillinger assembled a new gang, including gunman Lester Gillis ("Baby-Face" Nelson), and after a series of robberies, he decided to hide out at a quiet Wisconsin resort and fishing camp called Little Bohemia. Someone tipped off the FBI, and Melvin Purvis, the head of the FBI office in Chicago, moved dozens of agents from Chicago and St. Paul to the forests of Wisconsin. They raided the lodge on April 22, and federal agents killed one man and wounded two others—off-season fishermen with no connection to Dillinger.

The Little Bohemia fiasco put Purvis and J. Edgar Hoover under the harsh glare of public criticism. They became even more determined to catch Dillinger, and Hoover placed a shoot-to-kill order on the bandit's head, along with a $10,000 reward. Another $10,000 was offered by five states in which Dillinger had planned bank robberies. The newspapers screamed "Dillinger" every day, and over the course of the next couple of months, half a dozen men who resembled the bank robber were arrested or almost shot. The FBI and local authorities in Chicago and all over Illinois, Wisconsin, Minnesota and Indiana were looking everywhere for the elusive outlaw.

But plans had already been set in motion for Dillinger's demise. In early July 1934, Detective Sergeant Martin Zarkovich, of the notoriously corrupt East Chicago, Indiana police department, approached Chicago police captain John Stege with a deal that he wanted for a longtime friend and whorehouse madame named Anna Sage. She was in danger of being deported, and in return for being allowed to stay in the country, she claimed that she could deliver John Dillinger to the Chicago police. Stege kicked Zarkovich out of his office, so the detective went to see Melvin Purvis. The FBI official agreed, as long as Anna Sage could really deliver Dillinger. Ultimately, though, Sage would end up being shipped back to Europe as an "undesirable" in 1936.

When Dillinger walked into the Biograph Theatre on the night of July 22, 1934, Anna Sage promised her FBI contacts that she would be wearing a red dress (actually, it turned out to be bright orange) for identification purposes. She would be accompanying Dillinger, along with his newest girlfriend, Polly Hamilton Keele. At about 8:30 p.m., Dillinger appeared at the Biograph's box office in the company of two women. He was outfitted in a light summer suit, white canvas shoes and a straw boater hat. He seemed to be completely at ease.

Sixteen FBI agents, cops from East Chicago and Detective Martin Zarkovich waited outside the theatre with Purvis for more than two hours, watching for the unknowing Dillinger to exit. Purvis paced nervously, chain-smoked cigarettes and, several times, even entered the darkened theatre to be sure that Dillinger was still in his seat. Just before 10:30 p.m., the lights came up, the doors opened and the crowd filed out into the street. Finally, Dillinger left the theatre and was spotted by Melvin Purvis, who was standing in front of the Goetz Country Club, a tavern just south of the Biograph.

As Dillinger walked past him, Purvis struck a match to light his cigar, a signal for the FBI agents and the East Chicago policemen to go after their target. Glancing up the street, Purvis was shocked to see that two of the East Chicago cops had not seen the signal. They had been distracted by several Chicago plainclothes detectives who arrived on the scene. Detective Zarkovich, who saw what was happening, hurried across the street to his men. Meanwhile, two FBI agents were just finishing showing their credentials to the Chicago officers when they spotted the action outside the Biograph. They immediately started toward Dillinger.

Dillinger—Dead or Alive!

As all of this was taking place, Dillinger allegedly sensed that something was wrong. Polly later reported that she felt his arm tense. He scanned the area around him and slipped a hand into his pocket, where a gun had been hidden. He knew the alley up ahead was his best chance for escape, so he picked up his pace.

If Dillinger had any doubts about what was about to happen, they disappeared when he reached the mouth of the alley. Several men had fallen into step behind him, and he saw two men up ahead with guns in their hands. Moving forward, he turned his head to try and look behind him, and then, turning the girls loose, he tried to run. As he clawed for the gun in his pocket, he collided with a woman outside the alley and was spun halfway around. He grabbed at the woman and then shoved her away, realizing that she was a civilian. The assassins didn't hesitate over the woman's presence, and they immediately opened fire.

One slug burned through Dillinger's chest at a sideways, downward angle and punched out beneath his left rib. The second slammed into the base of his neck, ripped through his brain and exited beneath his right eye. The impact of the bullets, following his collision with the woman on the street, caused him to spin around like a top. FBI agents continued to fire five more times as Dillinger went down in the alley. None of the last bullets struck him, but they splintered a telephone pole that was a short distance behind him.

Dillinger stumbled and then collapsed, falling hard onto his face and elbow. A lens in his eyeglasses shattered and the brim of his straw hat snapped in two. His Colt revolver, its safety still on, was gripped in his fist. Melvin Purvis reached down and took it from his hand. One of his agents leaned down and heard the man on the ground try to speak. He mumbled a few incoherent words and then fell silent.

It was later recalled that a long moment of silence seemed to follow the shooting, and then chaos broke out. As Dillinger's blood spilled out onto the pavement, automobiles and streetcars came to a halt on North Lincoln Avenue. Passengers, followed by nearby pedestrians, poured into the street, all pushing for a closer look. Within moments, people were shouting the name, "Dillinger!"

Above the clamor, the screams of two women could be heard. The first, Etta Natalsky, was the woman Dillinger had bumped into. A stray bullet, from the gun of either an FBI agent or an East Chicago cop, had passed through the fleshy part of her thigh. The second injured woman was Theresa Paulus, who had been leaving the Biograph with a friend when a bullet from the other direction had clipped her in the hip. Neither one was seriously hurt, but once again, the FBI had claimed civilian casualties while hunting Dillinger.

Two of the agents crossed the alley and ducked into a Chinese restaurant to place a telephone call and announce that Dillinger was dead. They officially informed the local cops that the Department of Justice had "made an arrest" outside the Biograph Theatre.

Back outside, several of the agents hovered over the body as others tried to keep back the surging crowd. Agent Grier Woltz, who had been stationed next to Dillinger, later reported that Dillinger was "still kicking and moving around" on the pavement. He estimated that he lived about three minutes after the shooting and took one last shuttering breath before he died. No one did anything to try and help him.

Polly Hamilton and Anna Sage melted into the crowd and disappeared.

A few minutes later, a police van appeared on North Lincoln Avenue. Agent Woltz assisted as Dillinger's bloody body was lifted onto a stretcher, carried to the van and placed on the floor in back. Five FBI agents climbed in, along with three Chicago cops, and the body was taken to the Alexian

John Dillinger's death site.

Dillinger—Dead or Alive!

Brothers Hospital on Belden Avenue. Dr. Walter Prusaig turned them away at the door. He placed a stethoscope to Dillinger's chest and announced that he was dead. He didn't want the body brought inside, creating more confusion. Finally, a Chicago police detective ordered the body to be taken to the Cook County Morgue on Polk Street. Mobs greeted Dillinger's corpse at the morgue, but the scene at the Biograph Theatre remained chaotic. Spectators mobbed Lincoln Avenue outside the theatre. Tradition tells that passersby ran to the scene and dipped their handkerchiefs in the blood of the fallen man, hoping for a macabre souvenir of this terrible event. Others pried bullet fragments from a wooden light pole in the alley until the pole became so unsteady that it had to be removed by city workers.

The "extra" additions of the newspapers were already on the streets. The *Chicago Daily News* reported, "John Dillinger died tonight as he lived, in a hail of lead and swelter of blood. He died with a smile on his lips and a woman on each arm."

THE WRIGLEYVILLE
TORSO MURDER

C hicago is a city that has long been plagued by strange and unusual
crimes, but there is probably no murder as bizarre as the so-called "torso
murder" that occurred on the city's North Side in 1935. This blood-soaked
and grisly murder was made all the more strange by the cast of characters
involved, including a desperate mother in love with her daughter's husband,
a sickly young woman, her unwitting spouse and a former burlesque dancer
and coldblooded killer.

Chicagoans were shocked and horrified when details of the complicated
case reached the newspapers, but as usual, they clamored for more. And, as
is always the case in Chicago, the press was happy to oblige.

The story of the "torso murder" began in a backyard flat on West
Waveland Avenue in the Wrigleyville neighborhood. The small apartment
belonged to Blanche Dunkel, a semi-attractive, forty-two-year-old survivor
of four failed marriages. She shared it with her daughter, Mallie, and son-
in-law, Ervin J. Lang, a grocery store clerk who could not afford a place
for himself and his wife during the Depression. Mallie was a delicate
young woman with a "weak constitution," and she was unable to work.
Blanche largely supported the family by working in the linen supply room
of Passavant Hospital.

Blanche was a hard worker, but she was not terribly bright. She had
managed to make it most of the way through the eighth grade before she
dropped out of school, and newspapers later reported that she had an IQ of
seventy-nine. It's likely that she had some additional mental issues as well,
which would be evidenced by the events to come.

Living in close quarters in the cluttered apartment, Blanche soon found
herself falling in love with her daughter's charming husband. She described
his nature as "gentle and refined" and mistook his kindnesses toward her as
something other than innocent affection for his wife's mother. She was later

One of the greatest landmarks on Chicago's North Side is Wrigley Field, home of the Chicago Cubs. It is from the ballpark that the neighborhood of Wrigleyville takes its name. *Courtesy of the Library of Congress.*

quoted by the *Chicago Daily Times* as saying, "My God, it was selfish of me but no one will ever understand the thrill I got when I looked at that boy." Blanche constantly fantasized about Ervin making love to her. "I had to fight with myself to control my anger," Blanche said, "when I saw him with her."

Mallie Lang soon began to notice the extra attention that her mother was paying to Ervin and the way that she mooned over him whenever she thought Mallie wasn't looking. She and Blanche began to argue, and Mallie threatened to move out if her mother persisted with her foolish crush. Blanche angrily dared her to leave, knowing there was no way that the young couple could afford their own flat. Blanche even went as far as to borrow some money from friends to give to Mallie as a deposit for the first month's rent in an apartment of her own. Mallie gave up on her threat to leave. She felt trapped, but she knew that she and Ervin could not afford to move out. To make matters worse, Mallie's health, which had never been good to start with, was failing. Some days she was barely able to get out of bed. All that she could do was to try and ignore her mother's behavior, but it was becoming increasingly harder to do.

The Wrigleyville Torso Murder

One night at a neighborhood party, Blanche saw Ervin sitting quietly, holding Mallie's hand. She later recalled in an interview with the *Chicago Daily Times*:

> *Something came over me, something I don't understand. I jumped up from the table and ran over to him and smothered him with kisses. I was sorry then, she was already ill. And at the same time I wanted her to suffer because she had made me suffer—making me jealous.*

Blanche began working harder and harder to seduce her son-in-law. Eventually it worked, and Ervin succumbed to her advances. No one knows how she finally succeeded, but it's thought that perhaps she used the fact that Mallie had been too weak to engage in relations with her husband for a very long time. Whatever happened, Ervin found himself ravishing Blanche on every occasion Mallie was away from the house—and sometimes when she wasn't.

It all became too much for the delicate young woman to take. Mallie's health continued to decline, and she died, some say from a "broken heart," on December 20, 1934.

The simple-minded Blanche was shattered by her daughter's death and began her descent into madness. She began to blame herself for the fact that Mallie had died and turned her frenzied hatred toward Ervin. He had wasted no time in tossing the older woman aside and finding a new lover. He began to date a woman closer to his own age, a twenty-one-year-old named Josephine McKinley, who had a young son. Blanche, likely delusional by this time, imagined that Ervin had killed Mallie in order to start seeing Josephine, a woman he had never met before Mallie's death. Blanche was simply lying to herself. She had really wanted Ervin for herself, but he had quickly lost interest in her. She would later claim that her hate for Ervin was not because he had broken things off with her but because he had failed to remain loyal to the memory of his late wife.

Half crazed with jealously, Blanche took her suspicions about Ervin murdering Mallie to her sister, Mrs. Jessie Langdon. Her sister then put her in touch with a woman named Evelyn Smith, a laundry worker at the Medinah Club. Smith was a retired striptease dancer, and she became the strangest figure in this odd collection of characters. Her weird past was later revealed to investigators in the case.

Smith was born in Berlin, Germany, and was brought to North Dakota at a young age. Soon after arriving, her father died from pneumonia and her sister burned to death in a horrible "bonfire accident." Her mother went mad with grief and died herself a short time later. Evelyn was sent to live with a foster family, but she did not stay with them for long. At the age of ten, she began riding the rails of America, traveling in boxcars and living the life of a hobo. In the big cities, she wound up wherever there was a Chinatown district, thanks to the fact that the Chinese were always willing to provide shelter and food.

In 1929, Evelyn and another traveling woman ended up in Minneapolis, where they learned the laundry trade. Three years later, Evelyn drifted to Chicago and met a man named Harry Jung. He and his brothers had established a successful chain of laundries, and Evelyn saw him as the perfect "mark," a man she could con into providing her with a comfortable living. After a short acquaintance, they were married.

But Evelyn could not have been more wrong about Jung. He had plenty of money, but he wasn't willing to share it with his new wife. After she suffered a miscarriage, Jung forced her to go out and look for work. She supported herself through a series of odd jobs and eventually began dancing in a burlesque house under the stage name of "Trixie." Her striptease career was short-lived, mostly thanks to the fact that Evelyn was a plain-looking woman with a rough face, wire-rimmed glasses and auburn hair that she kept close-cropped like a man's. She was living in an apartment near the intersection of Clark and West Barry when she first met Blanche Dunkel.

Smith later claimed that she "fell under the spell" of Blanche when they met, and she was eager to help her out of the situation that she was in with Ervin. The police files in the case allude to the fact that Evelyn was a lesbian and that the "spell" she was under was one of sexual attraction. She had fallen for Blanche and would do anything to win her over. A short time later, she asked Jessie Langdon why Blanche didn't just have Ervin killed. "I could get it done for $500," she told her. Evelyn was by now very familiar with the inner workings of Chicago's South Side, and she offered the services of her husband and his associates for a sum of money that she knew Blanche would be able to obtain.

Blanche was able to get the money, and she got it from an unbelievable source—Ervin himself! She approached Lang's naïve little brother William for a key to the safe deposit box that Ervin kept at the Lake View Trust & Savings Bank. She withdrew $100 of Ervin's own money as a down payment for his murder. Blanche met Evelyn at the corner of Belmont and Lincoln and handed her a plain brown envelope with the cash inside. Evelyn instructed Blanche to bring the young man over to her house that evening.

That evening, Blanche managed to entice Ervin over to Evelyn's apartment with the promise of a night of drinking and card playing. Over the course of a few hours, he was served four whiskey highballs, each of which contained knockout drops. The women waited until nearly 4:30 a.m. before he finally passed out. Irritated and impatient, Evelyn slapped him hard across the face to see if he was really unconscious or if he had just nodded off. Satisfied that he would not wake up, Evelyn sent Blanche on her way. She promised to take care of Ervin from that point on. "You might as well go home," she reportedly said, according to the *Chicago Daily Times*. "I got him now."

Blanche, as filled with regret as she had been about hurting her daughter, fled the apartment. Meanwhile, Evelyn dosed Ervin with ether, tied him securely and then dragged him into a closet, where she strangled him to death. The next morning, Harry Jung arrived with a saw, and the two of them set to their bloody work. Evelyn cut off Ervin's legs at the hip so that he would fit into a large trunk that Jung had purchased at a Salvation Army store. They loaded the trunk into Jung's car and then set out for the southeast side, eventually crossing into Indiana to leave Ervin's legs in a roadside ditch near Munster. They took the torso to Wolf Lake, which straddles the Illinois-Indiana border, and dumped the remains into one of the many swampy areas nearby. The newspapers referred to the lake as a "gangland cemetery" because of the number of bodies that had been dumped there over the years.

Evelyn and Jung were sure that the body would never be found, but the severed corpse was discovered just four days later. The trunk that had been used to transport the body was found in a Chinatown warehouse at 231 West Twenty-second Street.

Once Ervin's body was identified, the police began to investigate, and the first break in the case came within twenty-four hours. Blanche's sister, Jessie Langdon, told Chief Investigator Thomas Kelly of the state's attorney police about Blanche's hiring of Evelyn Smith to kill Ervin. The unmistakable smell of laundry soap on Ervin's clothing confirmed the story and led the police to the Jung laundry business. Harry Jung vanished, but Evelyn was arrested in New York two weeks later.

Blanche was arrested and freely admitted to her part in the crime. She confessed after being taken out to Wolf Lake to view the remains. "I am his common-law wife," she said, imagining that their relationship had gone much further than it had. She continued to talk of how much she loved the young man as the police led her away to jail.

State's attorney Charles S. Doughtery easily convinced a grand jury to return murder indictments against Blanche and Evelyn. "I am ready for the chair," Evelyn sighed wearily in a public statement after the indictments were handed down. "It's better than putting up with all that happened. It wouldn't break my heart, though, if Blanche walks up to the chair with me." The news reporter from the *Chicago Daily Times* went on to add that "Mrs. Dunkel anticipated the prospect of death with different feelings."

Police officers search for clues in a drainage ditch at Wolf Lake, which became known in the 1920s and 1930s as a "gangland cemetery" thanks to the number of bodies that were found dumped there. *Courtesy of the* Chicago Daily News.

The judge at their trial, Cornelius J. Harrington, did not sentence the women to death, however. He felt that it was too good for them. Instead, he imposed a 180-year sentence to be served at the Dwight Reformatory for Women. He added another grim addendum to the sentence. Beginning on July 6, 1936, and for every year after, the women were ordered to spend the anniversary of Ervin's murder in solitary confinement.

In 1955, on the twentieth anniversary of the murder, a reporter for the *Chicago American* visited the two women in Dwight. Blanche, who was now sixty-three, held a Bible and praised Jesus a number of times throughout the interview. She had devoted her life to the Lord, she said, and had great remorse for the act that she had committed.

Evelyn Smith, however, was unrepentant. She told the reporter that her conscience was clear and her only interest in life these days was growing flowers. In the past twenty years, the only visitor to Evelyn's cell, except for the reporter, was a Catholic priest. She had turned him away.

Blanche was paroled from Dwight on March 6, 1961, with a final discharge from Governor Otto Kerner three years later. Evelyn was also paroled, more than a year later, on December 12, 1962. The two "women from hell," as the cops dubbed them, were now senior citizens, and both vanished from history, leaving a dark stain on the annals of crime in Chicago.

THE MURDER OF DR. PEACOCK

O ne of the North Side's most heartbreaking and puzzling murders occurred in early January 1936 with the brutal slaying of Dr. Silber Charles Peacock, one of Chicago's most respected physicians. The strange case was made even more confusing by the fact that there was not a hint of scandal or impropriety linked to the forty-year-old doctor's name, and despite the fact that his killers were eventually captured, there are a number of questions that remain unanswered, even after all of these years.

Dr. Peacock was born near Beverly in Adams County, Illinois, in 1896 and received his early education there. During World War I, he served in the U.S. Army Intelligence unit and worked closely with British Naval Intelligence. When he returned from the war, he attended Knox College in Galesburg, where he met his wife, Ruth Pearce, who was also a student. He graduated from Knox College in 1922 and was married after graduating from Rush Medical College in Chicago. He then interned at the Presbyterian Hospital before going into private practice. For ten years prior to his death, he spent countless hours researching deadly childhood diseases like scarlet fever and diphtheria and maintained a suite of offices in the Uptown National Bank building at 4753 Broadway with three other well-known physicians. He was also on the staff of the Children's Memorial, Henrotin and Ravenswood Hospitals. By 1936, Dr. Peacock, his wife and their seven-year-old daughter, Betty Lou, lived at the fashionable Edgewater Apartments at 5555 North Sheridan Road, one of the finer addresses on the North Side.

Peacock was a man of regular habits, but he was also considered one of the most skillful doctors in the city in the field of pediatrics, which made him often in demand. He was on call twenty-four hours a day, and in those days, it was not uncommon to be called to the bedside of a sick child at unusual times. Peacock was in the process of no longer accepting house calls, which made what happened on the night of his death even stranger.

On the night of January 2, Peacock picked up his wife, who was pregnant with their second child, and his daughter from Union Station. The first of what would be two mysterious telephone calls reached his apartment building switchboard at 7:30 p.m. The caller was a woman, and she refused to leave her name with the operator. At the time of the call, the Peacocks were having dinner at a North Side restaurant. His wife and daughter had just returned from a funeral in Bowen, Illinois, which was Ruth's hometown. They had gone to dinner after Dr. Peacock had picked them up from the train station.

Ruth and her daughter were anxious to settle in for the evening when they finally reached home, but for some reason, Dr. Peacock stepped out of the house about 8:30 p.m. When they arrived at the apartment, the switchboard operator stated that a call had come in for the doctor earlier in the evening, but the caller had not left a name. Could he have been returning a call? No one knows for sure, but it is known that he did make a telephone call from the pay phone in the drugstore that was located in the lobby of the apartment building. There is no indication as to why he left to make the call when there was a telephone in the apartment. This is just one of the lingering mysteries in the case.

A few minutes later, Dr. Peacock returned to his family's apartment and started to get ready for bed. He was in his pajamas when the telephone rang at 10:15 p.m. The switchboard operator later said that the caller was a man. Mrs. Peacock did not hear the voice of the caller, but she recalled afterward the words of her husband's side of the conversation: "The name...G. Smale, 6438 North Whipple Street...a sick child...the telephone number...Oh no, the telephone...usually five dollars...yes." Dr. Peacock scrawled the name and address of the caller on a piece of paper near the telephone.

Peacock quickly dressed, grabbed his coat and left the apartment. It was the last time that his wife saw him alive. When he had still not returned home by 1:30 a.m., Ruth made a frantic call to Cook County state's attorney Thomas Courtney, who was a personal friend of the Peacocks. The police were notified of the situation, and a missing persons report was filed. According to the *Chicago Tribune*, this might not have been the first bogus emergency call made to a doctor. In 1933, Dr. Benjamin Garnitz was lured from his home by a fake call and was shot to death by three young robbers. This must have been a concern of the police when they got the call about Dr. Peacock that night.

The Murder of Dr. Peacock

Detectives from the Summerdale district tracked down "G. Smale," whose name Dr. Peacock had written on the paper, but he lived at 6438 South Washtenaw Avenue, sixteen miles from the address on Whipple, literally at the opposite end of the city. Neither Smale nor the seven families who resided in an apartment at the Whipple address knew Dr. Peacock.

However, Peacock did apparently arrive at the building. Two of the tenants, Ben Noble and Mrs. Goldman, said that they heard an automobile outside of the apartment house at about 10:30 p.m. on that Thursday evening. A car door slammed, there was the sound of footsteps in the snow and then voices in the lobby of the building. Shortly afterward, both witnesses reported two slamming automobile doors and the car's motor as it drove away. If it was Dr. Peacock who drove up to the apartment building, whom had he met there and did that person leave with him? Detectives found six crushed cigarette butts and a discarded matchbook outside of the Whipple Street building, making them believe that someone had been impatiently waiting for the doctor's arrival. Did he hurt, or kill, Peacock when he arrived?

Another bit of information that puzzled the detectives was given to them by Dr. Peacock's private secretary, Katherine Maloney. She told them that Peacock rarely ever answered a night call from a patient, and when he did, it had to be one of his regular clients, since he was not accepting new patients at the time. In addition, when he did go out, his fee for such a call was usually seven dollars, although he had mentioned the amount of five dollars in the phone conversation that his wife overheard. Why would he have gone out on this night?

Twenty-one hours passed, and then a young man named Jack Dietrich noticed a parked car with its headlights on in front of a three-story building at 6236 North Francisco. Dietrich went over and peered in the window. Inside the car, he saw the lifeless form of Dr. Peacock hunched over the steering wheel. The contents of his medical bag were spread across the front seat. He had been murdered by two gunshots to the head and seven separate knife wounds. According to a coroner's report, Peacock had fought his killers. The knuckles of both his hands were bruised and swollen, as though he had struck several blows with his fists, and a rail behind the front seat of the car had been cracked, apparently after being struck with a heavy object. Detectives surmised that a hard blow had been aimed at Dr. Peacock's head and hit the rail instead. No bullets were found in the car, but there were bloodstains on the hand throttle and the instrument panel. The police believed that Dr. Peacock had been killed in the car but that the killer had driven it after his hands were stained by the doctor's blood.

The police believed that the violent nature of the crime suggested that the killer had a personal motive, and they began investigating from that angle. Investigators pursued the idea that perhaps the doctor had been killed by a patient, or a patient's parent, out of revenge, so all of his files were taken from his office to the Summerdale police station so detectives could go through them. There were so many questions in the case that detectives hardly knew where to begin.

Who disliked the physician enough to want to kill him? As far as everyone could tell, the young doctor had many friends and no enemies to speak of. He was a beloved children's doctor and was respected by everyone the police interviewed.

What was the significance of the name "Smale" and the address of "6438." Peacock had been lured out of his home to an address on North Whipple Street, and yet the only "G. Smale" in the city lived at 6438 South Washtenaw, at the other end of the city. The real G. Smale was interviewed by the police and not only offered a verifiable alibi, but he also did not know Dr. Peacock. He gave the police a list of every person he had given his business card to, but the lead came up empty.

Who was the woman who had called the Peacocks' apartment at 7:30 p.m. on the night of his death? To whom did Peacock speak when he made a call from the pay phone in the drugstore of the apartment building's lobby? Who had made the mysterious "mercy call" at 10:15 p.m. that night?

Why did Dr. Peacock rush out to answer the call when he usually referred night calls to other doctors and only accepted emergencies from his own patient list?

Was Dr. Peacock killed by someone who knew him? Or was he lured to his death by thieves? During a canvass of the area around Whipple and Devon, police spoke to a woman named Mrs. Helen Meyers, who told of riding past a car resembling Peacock's at the corner of Whipple and Devon about 10:30 p.m. on Thursday night. As the driver of her car slowed down to look at a street sign, she said that she noticed two men lurking nearby who "looked like robbers."

The mystery deepened when a friend of the doctor, Reverend Dr. Kenneth A. Hurst, told police that Peacock had two very influential enemies who wanted him dead. Hurst's wife was a cousin of Ruth Peacock and on good terms with the family. Dr. Peacock had dined with the Hursts while his wife and daughter were out of town, which is when he had told his friend about his personal problems. One of the enemies was a man named Arthur St. George, who allegedly accused Peacock of performing an illegal abortion on his wife, Arlene Johnson Thompson. But when investigators brought St. George in for questioning, they found this was not the case at all. Apparently,

The Murder of Dr. Peacock

Dr. Peacock had been kind to his wife, and Arlene had mistaken his kindness for something more than it was. She had left her husband as a result—or so St. George believed. Arlene denied everything, and the police found nothing in her story to suggest adultery as a possible motive for the doctor's murder. The newspapers played up what was thought to be a compelling lead for days, but in the end, nothing came of it.

The killer of Dr. Peacock remained at large.

The real killers turned out to be four teenage street criminals who had killed the doctor for twenty dollars and the sheer thrill of murder. The killers—Robert Goethe, Durland "Jimmy" Nash, Michael Livingston and Emil Reck—were arrested almost by accident. The police knew nothing of their connection to the Peacock murder until accounts of their past crimes began to unravel, including the murder of a tailor named Peter Payor and the beating of an elderly man named Matthew Holstein and his daughter, Christine, during a home robbery. Two police officers had run into Jimmy Nash on the street on March 25 and had questioned him about a missing girl named Doris Robbins. She was the third girl to go missing on the North Side in a matter of weeks. The other two girls were Evelyn Tveden and Patsy Dean, who was allegedly dating Nash at the time. The cops believed that the young man knew something about her disappearance. When questioned about Doris Robbins, the police officers didn't like Nash's answers, so they took him to the West North Avenue police station. There, after questioning, Nash said that he didn't know where Doris was but that he remembered meeting her at his friend Robert Goethe's house.

Goethe, Livingston and Reck were also brought in for questioning, and the police began connecting them to other crimes in the area, including the robbery of several doctors who had been lured out into the night by phony emergency calls. With the Peacock case still being actively worked, detectives were quick to make the connection. The young men quickly confessed to the murder, although Emil Reck had to be taken to the hospital after his confession. The *Chicago Tribune* reported that an old stomach ulcer began to bleed, forcing him to be placed under medical care. However, it would later be learned that Reck's bleeding came after he was severely beaten in the interrogation room—a common method of obtaining confessions in those days. All three of the boys had been shuttled back and forth between police stations all night, and Reck, who was partially retarded with the intelligence of a child of about ten, began vomiting up blood after repeated blows to the chest and abdomen.

According to the confessions, the four teenagers had met at Phil's Pool Room on Division Street a few hours before the killing. Goethe had looked through a classified telephone book to find a doctor on the North Side. They had already committed similar robberies and believed that a doctor on the lakeshore might carry more money with him. Dr. Peacock had been picked at random, and the first time they called, he was not home. It is believed that the switchboard operator thought that it was a woman calling because of the high-pitched voice of one of the teenage boys. Goethe called again. This time, he spoke with the doctor and told him that he needed help with a sick child. Nash, who was the first to confess, could not explain how Goethe had picked the address and name. He only knew that the other boy had once lived in that neighborhood and may have remembered it in that way. The boys had stolen a car, and after luring Dr. Peacock from his residence, he was beaten and shot to death on Whipple Street after putting up a terrible struggle.

After taking the twenty dollars that the man had in his wallet, Nash told the doctor to walk with them to his car. According to the *Chicago Tribune*, Nash told police:

> *This started him to fighting. Gee, he was tough. I hit him with the butt of my gun. Livingston slugged him with his fist. Reck took a knife out of the medicine case and slashed the doctor on the head with it. None of those things stopped him. He hit all of us and kicked Goethe in the groin. He got so tough that Goethe shot him in the head. He went down but he got up again, still battering and hollering: "Don't shoot me, don't shoot me." I clouted him on the head again and this time he passed out.*

The boys decided not to leave the body in front of the Whipple Street apartment building because it would be found too soon. They wrapped the doctor in his overcoat and bundled him into his car, which three of the boys drove to Francisco Avenue, where it was eventually discovered. Livingston followed in the gang's stolen car and they drove away. According to the *Tribune*, Nash said that he later asked Goethe why they had to kill this doctor when they had only robbed all of the others, and he replied, "I been to Bridewell [the new Cook County Jail that had been built in 1929] and I ain't going back again."

It was soon learned that Robert Goethe was the son of Rose Kasallis, a brothel madame who was sitting in the county jail after being arrested for running teenage prostitutes and a "school for crime" out of her apartment at 1339 North Maplewood. It came out during the trial that she had plied her son and his friends with alcohol and women and that she was a cunning promoter of theft, vandalism and murder. When she was arrested, the police had taken twenty-five of her girls away in a paddy wagon. In a statement

The Murder of Dr. Peacock

A map of the North Side showing the location of Dr. Peacock's residence, his office, the place where his body was found on Francisco Avenue and the address on Whipple Street where he was lured to his death. *Courtesy of the* Chicago Tribune.

from jail after her son's arrest, printed in the *Chicago Daily Times*, Rose cried that "Bobbie" was a "regular church-goer" who had never been in trouble.

Goethe and Nash both entered guilty pleas and accepted a sentence handed down by the court of 199 years in prison. During the trial for Livingston and Reck, it was established that Goethe had fired the fatal shots that killed Dr. Peacock but that Reck and Livingston—by their own admissions—had struck the doctor repeatedly. Assistant state's attorney John Boyle was demanding the death penalty against the boys, and with their guilt a foregone conclusion, defense attorneys shifted their arguments away from the crime itself and focused on what they claimed were illegal extortions of confessions by Chicago detectives. In addition to being beaten, they said, Emil Reck had been kept incommunicado and without the benefit of an attorney for nearly eighty hours. The jury was not impressed by their arguments. This was simply the way things had to be done in those days, and both Reck and Livingston were convicted on May 20, 1936, barely escaping the electric chair. Having had no active role in the murder, Livingston was sentenced to thirty years. Reck's punishment was set at 199 years, just like the other boys.

But the story of Emil Reck simply refused to go away. In 1961, the American Civil Liberties Union presented oral arguments to the U.S. Supreme Court on behalf of the mentally challenged man, and in a seven-to-two decision, the high court threw out Reck's confession and ordered the case to be retried. The new charges against Reck were dismissed for lack of evidence, bringing this strange and tragic case to a close—and leaving behind an impression of brutality and corruption that still haunts the Chicago police department to this day.

DEATH OF A SHOWGIRL

The horrific murder of Chicago showgirl Estelle Carey remains one of the Windy City's most heinous crimes. To this day, it remains unsolved, although many writers and police officers have linked the crime to the Chicago Outfit, believing that Estelle's death occurred because she simply knew too much.

On the early afternoon of February 2, 1943, firefighters responding to an alarm rushed into a trendy Gold Coast apartment at 512 West Addison Street. What they found inside was a scene of carnage and horror. In the apartment, they found the body of a dead woman partly concealed beneath an overturned chair, her feet and legs consumed by the flames. She had been battered with a blackjack, a kitchen rolling pin and a whiskey bottle, slashed by a bread knife and strangled. The coroner later determined that she had not died from the assault but from second- and third-degree burns from the fire.

Her body appeared to have been butchered. Matted hair was found next to her corpse by detectives who were soon called to the scene, but whose hair it was could not be determined by the police lab. It was obvious that the young woman had fought for her life because signs of a violent struggle were everywhere. There were bloodstains all over the apartment —on the stove, on the rear door through which the killer likely fled (the front door was still locked), on cabinet doors and all over the living room.

A variety of weapons had been used on her. Found scattered throughout the apartment were the bloody bread knife, an electric iron that was coated with blood, a blackjack and a broken whiskey bottle, its jagged edges streaked with gore. There were bloody smudges all over the house, but not a single fingerprint was found, other than those of the victim and her roommate, Maxine Buturff, who proved to be elsewhere at the time of the killing.

Investigators quickly learned that the name of the victim was Estelle Carey. She grew up on the North Side and had worked as a waitress and occasional model before taking a job at a swanky Rush Street nightclub. According to her cousin Phoebe, she had been home alone on the afternoon of February 2. With her roommate out for the day, Estelle decided to make a few telephone calls. She was chatting on the phone with Phoebe when the doorbell rang. Phoebe remembered hearing Estelle's little dog barking in the background, but Estelle did not seem concerned. Ending the call, she had apparently gone to the door and opened it for her killer.

Nightclub hostess and showgirl Estelle Carey, whose brutal murder was never solved. *Courtesy of Wide World Photos*.

Death of a Showgirl

When the cops interviewed Estelle's neighbors, they spoke with Mrs. Jessie Lovrein, who lived in the same building and said that she was looking out her back window at about 2:30 p.m. when she saw a man going down the rear stairs. She gave a vague description of the man, stating that after he left the rear of the apartment building, he walked across a snow-covered lot toward Lake Shore Drive. She added that he was carrying two fur coats. A check of Estelle's wardrobe revealed that a sable and a mink coat were missing.

Strangely, though, more than $2,500 in jewelry that Estelle kept in a shoebox was untouched, along with the key to her safe deposit box. The box later yielded about $2,000 in cash, bonds and jewelry. Whatever the killer had been looking for, it had apparently not been money.

The initial police investigation focused on jealous lovers. Estelle had plenty of suitors from working at the club, evidenced by a pile of steamy letters found stashed in her bedroom. With the coats missing, the police surmised that the fire had been set to cover a robbery. But if robbery was the motive, why leave the jewelry behind? As more digging was done into Estelle's background, detectives began to uncover her strong connections to Chicago's underworld, notably to a local hood named Nick Circella (aka Nick Dean). It was because of Circella that Estelle Carey became involved in one of the most deadly mob scandals of the early 1940s.

When Al Capone was convicted of income tax evasion and was sent off to prison, the Chicago Outfit expanded in a number of directions. Prohibition was over, and the mob began looking toward gambling, prostitution and extortion as major rackets. One extortion scheme stretched all the way to Hollywood.

In the early 1930s, two minor Chicago labor racketeers, Willie Bioff and George E. Browne, began extorting money from local theatre owners. Under the guise of donating money to area soup kitchens to feed the city's Depression victims, the two men hit up one theatre chain for $20,000. While celebrating this coup, Bioff and Browne got drunk and bragged about the scheme in front of Nick Circella. The two loudmouths soon became "employees" of the Chicago Outfit.

With the backing of the Chicago mob, Browne became president of IATSE, the International Alliance of Theatrical Stage Employees and Motion Picture Operators. The membership consisted of motion picture employees, from stagehands and technicians in Hollywood to projectionists at local movie houses. Bioff and Browne extorted from, and dictated to, the biggest names in Hollywood's motion picture industry, including Louis B. Mayer and the Warner brothers.

On May 24, 1941, Bioff and Browne were indicted on federal racketeering charges in New York City, where many of the movie moguls maintained their business offices. The two were found guilty five months later, on October 30. Bioff was sentenced to ten years in prison; Browne, to eight. Each was fined $20,000. Nick Circella, who was indicted at the same time, pleaded guilty and received an eight-year sentence.

Prosecutors weren't satisfied with locking up the men they saw as only minor players in the mob. They wanted the top men in the organization, but the only way to get them was to convince Browne, Bioff and Circella to talk. Browne and Bioff were questioned relentlessly but refused to name names. Prosecutors then went after Nick Circella, who had originally gone to prison rather than submit to questioning and give up his associates. However, prosecutors found that prison life had eroded his determination, and he agreed to talk. Circella refused to spell out everything for them, but he did agree to cooperate to a degree and spent part of January 1943 in front of a New York grand jury. The mob in Chicago soon got word that Circella was talking.

The Chicago Outfit immediately began damage control procedures. First, mob emissaries approached Mrs. Circella and asked her to talk to her husband for them. In mid-January, while on a trip to New York, she met with Nick and pleaded with him not to say anything else. But his wife's appeals had little effect, and word came back to Frank Nitti and Paul Ricca, the top mob men in Chicago, that Circella planned to continue testifying for the grand jury. Nitti and Ricca were seen conferring with associates in a downtown hotel room in late January. The mob decided not to act against Mrs. Circella, but there was someone else they knew they could make an example out of.

Circella had been cozy with beautiful Estelle Carey since the mid-1930s. He had met her while she was still waiting tables and modeling, and Circella was so taken with her that he installed her in his swanky joint, the Yacht Club, a combination casino and nightclub near Rush Street.

Estelle's job was managing one of several "26" dice tables, a simple form of gambling in many clubs and taverns. Usually, an attractive woman like Estelle sat behind a green felt table, entertaining patrons who wagered less than one dollar at a time. A "26" game was really just a come-on game for potential gamblers. A client first selected his target number, one through six, from the dice cube. He placed his bet, then took a leather cup with ten cubes and rolled them out thirteen times. Each time, the hostess counted and marked the number of times his payoff number came up. The payoff odds depended on the final tally: totals of ten or less and thirty or more paid the highest, while odds with twelve or any number between fourteen and twenty-five were losers.

The key to Estelle's job was her ability to work with amusing, flirtatious gentlemen and lonely drunks, building a rapport and ensuring their future return, while also relieving them of ten dollars or more each night. The latter was achieved through skillful manipulation of the dice, which usually meant switching loaded dice into the game or marking a false tally in the house's favor. Estelle quickly proved to be quite good at this, allegedly scamming at least $800 from one customer. She also had a good eye for the high rollers and steered them away from the small games, directing them to the upstairs casino, where much more damage could be done.

Estelle became such a moneymaker for Circella that he made her the manager of all of the "26" games and reportedly gave her 25 percent of the take. Later, he moved her over to the ritzy Colony Club on Rush Street, where she increasingly handled a considerable portion of Circella's funds, some of it thought to be extortion and payoff money for which Nick was responsible. The two became lovers, and he kept her in expensive gowns, moved her into a high-class apartment and provided her with an income of more than $500 a week.

Estelle's good fortune should have come to an end in 1940, when police raids shuttered the Colony Club. After that, her benefactor was indicted in the Hollywood extortion case in 1941. When the FBI nabbed him, the obvious notion was that Estelle had given away his location. Seemingly unbothered by this, Estelle continued to be seen with several men about town, one of whom she vacationed with in Florida. She remained well-dressed, apparently not hurting financially after Circella was arrested. Talk turned to money that had gone missing, and one writer surmised that Estelle was safeguarding Nick's extortion money while he was away. Any mob suspicions regarding her role with the FBI in building the extortion case were likely well-founded because the feds intended to call her as a prospective witness. Further rumors of collaboration with the Internal Revenue Service didn't help her position.

Then, on February 2, 1943, Estelle Carey was brutally murdered. Had the mob finally caught up with her?

Police investigators thought so. Dozens of underworld suspects were interrogated and released. Two of the main suspects were Ralph Pierce and his friend Les "Killer" Kruse, but lacking solid evidence, the police had to release them.

Detectives came to believe that Estelle knew the location of Circella's syndicate money and was either keeping it or had hidden it somewhere

Estelle vacationed in Florida after Nick Circella was arrested. She was killed when she returned to Chicago in 1943. *Courtesy of Wide World Photos.*

herself. Her death involved torture, and they suspected that perhaps her attacker had tried to get her to give up the location of the money. Did she tell what she knew? No one would ever know, and what happened to Estelle Carey became merely a matter of endless speculation. The pretty young girl's killer was never found.

As an after note, the mob's strategy in killing Estelle Carey initially seemed to work. When the news of her death made it to New York, prosecutors lost Circella as a witness. As soon as he found out that she had been killed, he refused to offer any additional testimony.

The murder had a completely different effect on Bioff and Browne. Bioff especially was enraged. He immediately called in prosecutors. "We sit around in jail for those bastards and they go killing our families. To hell with them! What do you want to know?"

On March 18, 1943, another New York City grand jury handed down indictments on Frank Nitti, Paul "the Waiter" Ricca, Louis "Little New York" Campagna, Phil D'Andrea and others. Nitti, rumored to be despondent at the possibility of returning to prison, committed suicide the day after the indictments were announced.

If Nitti had been the man who ordered the death of Estelle Carey, as many seemed to believe, then perhaps this tragic woman got one last bit of revenge from beyond the grave.

"CATCH ME BEFORE I KILL MORE"

The case of the "Lipstick Killer" is one of the most intriguing stories in the annals of Chicago's postwar crime. Despite the fact that the police nabbed University of Chicago student William Heirens for the murders of the two women found slashed to death in their apartments near Wrigley Field, there are many crime buffs who believe that the real killer got away. Heirens may have been guilty of many things, but they believe that the killings of those two young women were not among them.

Those two North Side murders were not ordinary crimes, especially in the days before a term like "serial killer" was in common use. Each of the women had been savagely slain, and the killer had bathed their corpses. A message was found written in red lipstick on the wall at the second murder scene:

For heaven's sake, catch me before I kill more.

The police couldn't be sure if the killer was taunting them or genuinely crying for help. But before they could find out, the day came that has since become known as "the day Chicago locked its doors." On January 6, 1946, just twenty blocks north in the Edgewater neighborhood, a little girl was stolen from her bed in the middle of the night and cut into pieces that were found scattered all over the North Side of the city.

The police were desperate to find the killer and came to believe that all of these violent crimes were linked together. If they could find this horrible monster, they could bring an end to the wave of fear that was sweeping through the entire Windy City. When they finally arrested William Heirens, it seemed that the terror was finally over. But was it? That remains a matter of conjecture to this day.

The famous photo of "Lipstick Killer" William Heirens behind bars. He implored the police to "catch me before I kill more." *Courtesy of Wide World Photos.*

On June 6, 1945, the *Chicago Tribune* printed a small article about a woman named Josephine Ross who had been murdered in her apartment at 4108 North Kenmore Avenue, a building that overlooked Graceland Cemetery. According to the article, someone had entered her apartment while she was still sleeping and stabbed her to death. Her throat had been cut, and the killer washed the blood from her body in the bathtub. When he was finished, he taped her flesh back together with adhesive tape. The crime had been reported by Mrs. Ross's daughter, who had to pass a lie detector test to convince detectives that she had not staged the unusual crime scene.

As the investigation progressed, several of Ross's boyfriends and ex-husbands were questioned, but all of the leads quickly fizzled out. The victim had been found with several dark hairs clutched in her hand, and two witnesses stated that they had seen a dark-haired man leaving the scene, but aside from those details, there was little else to go on. Soon, the case went cold.

Six months later, on December 10, 1945, another woman was killed in her apartment, which was only five blocks away from the Ross apartment. Frances Brown, a former navy WAVE and an office worker at the A.B. Dick Company, was found dead in her apartment at 3941 North Pine Grove Avenue. The killer had gotten into her apartment late at night, climbing from a fire escape into her bedroom window, which was six stories above the street. Frances had been shot in the head and stabbed. The blade of the knife had been driven into her throat with such force that it came out the other side of her neck. The pretty young woman was found completely nude, but she had not been sexually violated. Chief of Detectives Walter Storm quickly noted the similarities between the murder of Frances Brown and that of Josephine Ross. In addition to being entered by the killer late at night, both apartments had been ransacked, but little was taken. The victims had both been stabbed to death, each body had been carefully washed in the bathtub and the wounds had been taped back together again.

But on the wall next to Frances Brown's bed, the police found words that had been written in the victim's lipstick. The crimson markings would be seared into the memory of the cops—and into the memory of every Chicagoan who picked up a newspaper the next day:

For heaven's sake, catch me before I kill more. I cannot control myself.

The Brown murder, now linked to the slaying of Josephine Ross, galvanized the city. Newspapers blared headlines about a new Jack the Ripper stalking the city and began calling him the Lipstick Killer. Detectives began rounding up sex offenders, deviants and mental cases, but little progress was made. The only bit of physical evidence that had been left behind at the scene was a single fingerprint smudged onto a doorjamb. Unfortunately, it didn't match any of the prints the police had on file, and the fingerprint led to another dead end. It looked as though the only chance the authorities might have to catch the killer was if he committed another murder—and made a mistake.

A month later, the Lipstick Killer was replaced in the headlines by one of the greatest atrocities ever committed in Chicago. On January 6, 1946, seven-year-old Suzanne Degnan was kidnapped in the middle of the night. At some point after 9:00 p.m., her abductor had slipped into the window of the Degnan home at 5943 North Kenmore Avenue and had taken the little girl away. Her parents found her vanished, and the window of the bedroom standing open, the next morning. A scrawled ransom note was found on the floor of Suzanne's bedroom:

> *Get $20,000 reddy* [sic] *& waite* [sic] *for word.*
> *Do not notify FBI or police. Bills in $5's and $10's.*
> *Burn this for her safty* [sic].

Later that morning, a man telephoned the Degnan house several times, asking about the ransom money, but he hung up before any real conversation could take place.

Meanwhile, scores of policemen and volunteers scoured the North Side neighborhood, and just after dark that evening, an officer made a gruesome discovery. Behind a building on the west side of Kenmore, south of Thorndale, the policeman saw a catch basin that appeared to have been tampered with. When he lifted the lid and peered inside with his flashlight, he found the severed head of a little blond-haired girl floating in the water. The head belonged to Suzanne Degnan, and officers were alarmed as more body parts began to turn up. Suzanne's right leg was found in another catch basin in the same alley and her left leg in an alley east of Kenmore. Her torso was discovered in a storm drain at the northwest corner of Kenmore and Ardmore. Her arms would remain undiscovered until the following month, when they were found near Hollywood and Broadway.

The public was outraged by this new development. Not since the murder of Bobby Franks in 1924 (by thrill killers Leopold and Loeb) had Chicago seen such a terrible crime committed against an innocent child. The newspapers screamed for vengeance, and the police commissioner and the state's attorney both personally appeared at the Degnan home and vowed to capture whoever had carried out such a horrific crime and bring him to justice.

As the investigation continued, it was found that the kidnapper had taken Suzanne to an apartment building at 5901 North Winthrop Avenue, just a block from her home, and had dismembered her in a laundry room in the basement. Efforts had been made to clean up the scene, but investigators found traces of blood in a laundry tub. The police focused on anyone with access to the room, and the crudely written, badly misspelled ransom note led them to focus their attention on the building's sixty-five-year-old janitor, a Belgian named Hector Verburgh. Although tenants described him as a kindly old man, he was taken to the Summerdale district police station, and cops spent forty-eight hours trying to get a confession out of him. He refused to admit that he had anything to do with the crime.

On January 10, lawyers from the Janitor's Union managed to free Verburgh, and it was later determined that he could not write English well enough to have penned the ransom note. He sued the police for brutality and was eventually awarded $20,000.

Detectives started all over again, but new information soon came to light. On January 5, just one night before Suzanne was kidnapped, a burglary had occurred at an apartment near the Degnan home—an apartment that overlooked Suzanne's bedroom window. Not much had been taken during the break-in, other than a scrapbook of wartime photos, but detectives believed that if they could find the scrapbook, it might lead them to Suzanne's killer.

Months passed, and after several dead ends and false clues, the case grew cold. In late January, the police answered the question of the mysterious telephone calls that came into the Degnan house on the morning after Suzanne's abduction. Still working on the idea that the killer might have committed other crimes in the area, detectives routinely picked up ex-cons and petty criminals. In late January, they hauled in a neighborhood hoodlum named Theodore Campbell, who, under questioning, claimed to know who killed Suzanne Degnan. He told them it was Vincent Costello, another local punk who was well known to the police and lived only four blocks from the Degnan home.

According to Campbell, his buddy Costello had told him on January 7 that he had kidnapped the Degnan girl, killed her and disposed of her body. He wanted Campbell to call the Degnans and try to get a ransom from them. In light of the strange calls that had been made to the family that morning, the police had no reason not to believe the story. Costello was arrested and was interrogated all night.

By morning, though, the story had fallen apart. Lie detector tests indicated that neither Costello nor Campbell had any part in the murder, and eventually they admitted that they had overheard police officers talking about the case on the morning after the abduction and thought it would be fun to call the Degnan house as a prank. The mystery of the telephone calls had been solved, but investigators were no closer to finding the killer.

Hundreds more were questioned, but it was not until June 27 that another viable suspect appeared. On that day, a University of Chicago student named William Heirens was arrested following a burglary in Rogers Park. Two days later, he was the leading suspect in the murder of Suzanne Degnan—and soon was believed to be the Lipstick Killer as well.

William Heirens was born in 1928. He was raised and attended school all over the North Side. His parents grew flowers in a greenhouse on Chase

Avenue, just east of Western, until the Depression put them out of business. His father, George Heirens, tried his luck at a small flower shop downtown and then later became a security guard. William attended several Catholic grade schools as a child, including Saint-Mary-of-the-Lake Catholic School at 4200 North Kenmore, just a half block from where Josephine Ross would later be murdered.

When William was a teenager, the Heirenses' neighbors began noticing that women's undergarments had started disappearing from clotheslines and, later, from dresser drawers. Apparently, William was hiding them away to enjoy later. He outgrew his fascination with panties but did not outgrow his need to commit burglaries, soon stealing cash, jewelry, guns and more. When he was arrested the first time, he had managed to amass about $3,500 in loot. According to the *Chicago Tribune*, a psychiatrist who examined him for the juvenile court termed his compulsion for theft "neurotic stealing."

Many of Heirens's break-ins were committed with death-defying acts as he jumped from one building to another, high above the ground. He targeted apartment windows on high floors, seemingly without fear, and had a talent for climbing up walls that seemed impassable at first glance. During many of his robberies, he set fire to the apartments or defecated on the floor, unable to control the strange urges that seized him.

His first arrest was in June 1942 and came when police staked out a building on Sheridan Road that had been burglarized several times. Heirens was only thirteen years old at the time and still in the eighth grade. He confessed to ten other burglaries, which was only a fraction of the real number that he had committed. The *Tribune* called him a "one boy crime wave."

Instead of being sent to a reformatory, Heirens was allowed to attend Gibault, a privately run Catholic school in Indiana, where he stayed for the next year. He was a model student, and in June 1943, he was allowed to return home. His family had moved to 1020 West Loyola Avenue, which was six blocks from where Suzanne Degnan would later be murdered.

Unfortunately, his time at the private reform school had little positive effect on Heirens. On August 8, 1943, he was caught prowling around an apartment building near Pratt and Sheridan. According to the police, eight or nine of the apartments had been looted. This time, Heirens's mother, Margaret, convinced an inexperienced judge to send the boy to St. Bede School, about eighty miles southwest of Chicago. Even though the school does not usually admit students with a criminal record, Heirens was there until early 1945. Once again, he was a model student, and after his court supervision ended, he returned home to Chicago.

"Catch Me Before I Kill More"

After his second arrest, Heirens's parents decided that a more rural neighborhood—with fewer houses to burglarize—would benefit the young man. They rented a farmhouse at Touhy and Keeler Avenues, and George Heirens helped his son get a summer job as a laborer for the Illinois Central Railroad in downtown Chicago. Heirens traveled to work by catching the bus at Keller and taking it to the el station in Rogers Park. From there, he took the train downtown. On June 5, 1945, Heirens left home but never made it to work. The next morning, the newspapers reported the mysterious murder of Josephine Ross. She lived very close to the el line that Heirens took to get to work.

Although the courts didn't require it, Heirens's mother wanted him to return to St. Bede to finish high school. Heirens wanted to stay at home, but then he heard about a special program at the University of Chicago that allowed selected students to enter college early by taking a special exam. He scored well on the exam and, in September 1945, entered college as a sixteen-year-old freshman. His grades were better than average the first semester, but his studies didn't prevent him from committing more burglaries.

On October 5, 1945, an army WAC named Evelyn Peterson was assaulted in an off-campus apartment by an attacker who broke into her place through a skylight. The attack was interrupted when her sister knocked at the apartment door and the burglar fled. The sister reported seeing a suspicious stranger in the building that day, and in July 1946, she picked William Heirens out of a police lineup.

On June 26, 1946, Heirens was in desperate need of money and decided to cash in some of the bonds that he had stolen during his burglaries. He wanted to do this at a post office outside of the city, so he bought a ticket on the North Shore suburban train for Skokie. When he arrived, though, the post office was already closed. Unable to get money this way, he decided to steal some. He took the train back to the city and got off at the Morse Avenue station in Rogers Park. He quickly walked over to the Wayne Manor Hotel, an apartment building that had always been one of his favorite burglary spots. But things went wrong on this day when he walked into an unlocked apartment on the third floor and was confronted by a tenant who spotted him in the hall. As the alarm was sounded, Heirens ran for the stairs. When he reached the ground floor, he ran into a janitor, who tried to stop him. Heirens pulled out a revolver. The man stepped out of the way and watched Heirens bolt out of the front door and onto Wayne Avenue.

He ran south and ducked behind some buildings on the north side of Farwell. He found a partly enclosed porch at 1320 West Farwell and tried to hide there, but the woman who owned the house saw him and called the police. Officers Tiffin Constant and William Owens responded to the call and were joined by Abner Cunningham, an off-duty cop who lived down the street. As they approached, Heirens took out his revolver and attempted to pull the trigger, but the gun misfired. He tossed away the gun, jumped onto Officer Constant and began to struggle with him. Abner Cunningham, who was unarmed, picked up a stack of flower pots and smashed them over Heirens's head, knocking him unconscious.

Heirens was treated at Edgewater Hospital and then taken to the Cook County Jail. Although it seemed to be a minor arrest, a newspaper story about an unarmed cop who brought in a suspect by subduing him with a flower pot was picked up on the Associated Press wire and appeared in newspapers all over the country.

The following morning, police officers searched Heirens's dorm room at the University of Chicago. They found a hoard of items from an estimated twenty-five to fifty burglaries, including cameras, jewelry, thousands of dollars worth of bonds—and a scrapbook filled with photos of prominent Nazis. It was a war memento that belonged to a former soldier named Harry Gold, and it had been stolen from his apartment at 5959 North Kenmore Avenue during a burglary that occurred on January 5, 1946. This was the first piece of evidence possibly linking Heirens to the murder of Suzanne Degnan. It placed him on her block just twenty-four hours before she was killed, and homicide detectives had long suspected that whoever had burglarized the nearby apartment might be her killer.

Officers also found a gun that linked Heirens to a shooting in Rogers Park. The Colt revolver had been stolen from Guy Rodrick at 5000 South Cornell Avenue on December 13, 1945. Two days later, a housewife named Marion Caldwell was sitting in her kitchen at 1209 West Sherwin Avenue when someone fired a bullet through her window and wounded her in the face. The bullet would later be matched to the gun found in Heirens's dorm room.

At the time of the search, however, Heirens was not suspected of anything other than burglary. The officers on the scene inventoried everything they found and estimated the value of each item. The scrapbook was valued at one dollar and the Colt revolver was thought to be worth about five dollars.

When the Degnan ransom note had been found in January, the Chicago crime lab had been unable to lift any fingerprints from it, but the FBI, using more advanced techniques, was able to lift one clear print. Prior to Heirens's arrest, fingerprint expert Sergeant Thomas Laffey had compared it to more than seven hundred other prints with no luck—but his luck changed on June 28. The police were able to discover seven points of similarity between the fingerprint on the ransom note and the fingerprints of William Heirens. His prints also matched those found in the apartment of Evelyn Peterson, the woman who had been attacked in her off-campus apartment on Drexel Avenue.

At first, Sergeant Laffey had been unable to match Heirens to the bloody fingerprint found in the apartment of Lipstick Killer victim Frances Brown, but when a more complete set of prints was taken, which included the joints of his right forefinger, a match was made. The FBI confirmed the match on July 13.

While circumstantial, more links were found between Heirens and his possible victims when detectives began investigating his background. They learned that Heirens had lived near the Degnan home and also near both the Ross and Brown apartments. Although Frances Brown and the Degnan family lived nearly three miles apart, Heirens had burglarized homes on both of these blocks. To the investigators, it seemed hard to believe that this could be a coincidence. State's attorney William Touhy believed that they had the killer of Suzanne Degnan, Frances Brown and most likely Josephine Ross as well. He began building a case that would convince a jury of that fact.

Almost from the time of his arrest, Heirens claimed to be innocent of the murders. On the night of June 30, he asked to speak with Captain Ahern of the Rogers Park police district. He had known Ahern since the time he was first arrested at age fourteen and felt that he could trust him. He told Ahern that he had not committed the murders but suggested that a friend of his named George Murman may have been involved. He claimed that George had given him the loot that had been found in dorm room and that Heirens had just been holding it for him. The police searched for George Murman and questioned everyone Heirens knew about the man, but no one had heard of him, and no trace of anyone by that name could be found. They came to the conclusion that George Murman was an imaginary friend that Heirens had invented.

On July 9, Heirens was indicted for assault to murder Marion Caldwell of 1209 Sherwin Avenue and also for assault to murder the tenant who sounded the alarm and the janitor who confronted him at the Wayne Manor Hotel. He was also indicted for assault to kill Officer Constant, the cop who arrested him on June 26, and for twelve burglaries, including the apartment of Harry Gold at 5959 North Kenmore Avenue. On July 10, he was indicted for robbery and assault to kill Evelyn Peterson of South Drexel Avenue and for twelve additional burglaries, including one at the apartment of Guy Rodrick of 5000 South Cornell. Finally, on July 26, Heirens was indicted for the murders of Suzanne Degnan and Frances Brown.

George and Margaret Heirens didn't have much money, but they managed to hire a team of well-connected lawyers, the Coghlan brothers, to defend their son. The attorneys looked at the evidence that had been compiled against their young client, especially the fingerprint evidence that had been confirmed by the FBI and the burglary and assault indictments, which would carry substantial prison sentences on their own, and they recommended a plea bargain. George and Margaret Heirens agreed.

The Coghlans negotiated a favorable plea agreement that called for Heirens to plead guilty, write up a confession for the three murders and answer all of the questions that the state's attorney had for him. In return, he would receive essentially one life sentence for the murders, plus concurrent sentences for the other crimes. With good behavior, he would likely spend about twenty-five years in prison and could be out of prison by the 1970s. With his lawyer's assistance, Heirens wrote up the confession, and both he and his parents signed it. However, when the time came for him to answer the questions posed by the state's attorney, Heirens suddenly claimed that he couldn't remember anything. He simply refused to talk.

Left with no other choice, State's Attorney Touhy regarded the plea agreement to be nullified and announced that he would press ahead with a trial for the murders of Suzanne Degnan and Frances Brown.

There is no question that Heirens should have answered William Touhy's questions and taken the deal because his written confession contained a piece of information that had been previously unknown to the police. In the confession, he said that he had cut up Suzanne Degnan's body with a hunting knife and that he had gotten rid of the knife by tossing it up onto the el tracks from the alley behind Winthrop Avenue. No one had ever searched that spot.

When reporters from the *Chicago Tribune* learned of this, they immediately headed for the el tracks, arriving there before the police. They found a track maintenance man who told them that he had found a knife on the tracks on that area and, in fact, still had it in a storage room at the Granville el station. The reporters determined that a knife of the same description had been reported stolen from Guy Rodrick—the same Guy Rodrick who owned the Colt revolver that had been found in Heirens's dorm room. On July 31, Rodrick positively identified the knife as his own.

Even though no forensic evidence linked the knife to the murder, it was still a crucial piece of evidence against Heirens. Prior to its discovery, the prosecution had nothing to directly link him to the Degnan crime scene, aside from fingerprints on the ransom note. It would have been simple for the defense to claim that anyone could have written the note on paper that

"Catch Me Before I Kill More"

Heirens once touched. The knife was much harder to disregard, and State's Attorney Touhy felt that it was enough to put Heirens in the electric chair.

With that in mind, he offered Heirens one last plea bargain—three life sentences that would run consecutively. Heirens could escape execution, but he would never get out of prison. On the advice of his lawyers, Heirens took the new agreement. He answered the state's attorney's questions and reenacted the three murders in view of reporters. Captain Ahern from Rogers Park stated that he never believed that Heirens was the killer until he saw how familiar Heirens seemed to be with Frances Brown's apartment.

On September 4, with his parents and the victim's families in attendance, Heirens admitted his guilt on the burglary and murder charges. That night, he tried to hang himself in his cell, timed to coincide with a shift change of the prison guards, but he was discovered before he died. The following day, William was formally sentenced to three life terms in prison. According to Joseph Garinger in his book *William Heirens: Lipstick Killer or Legal Scapegoat*, as he waited to be transferred to Stateville Prison in Joliet, Cook County sheriff Michael Mulcahy asked Heirens if Suzanne Degnan suffered when she was killed. Heirens replied, "I can't tell you if she suffered, Sheriff Mulcahy. I didn't kill her. Tell Mr. Degnan to please look after his other daughter, because whoever killed Suzanne is still out there."

This was only the beginning of the claims that William Heirens did not commit the murders. In the years that have followed, Heirens has claimed that he was beaten and coerced into confessing to crimes that he didn't commit. Others have joined his efforts, pointing out how he passed a lie detector test in 1946, the suspicious nature of fingerprints that could not at first be matched, the flimsy nature of the circumstantial evidence, the inconsistencies in his confession and even alternative suspects that were released after Heirens confessed to the crimes. They believe that Heirens was nothing more than a convenient scapegoat, easily framed by the police who were under siege by the public and the press for their inability to find the real killer.

Is there any truth to the claim of Heirens's innocence? It's possible that it may be partially true—Heirens was almost assuredly the Lipstick Killer, but did he really murder Suzanne Degnan? The Lipstick Murders were obviously the work of one man, an experienced burglar who committed murder when he found that the apartment he was robbing was occupied. Heirens killed twice and may have been overwhelmed with guilt after the murder of Frances Brown, which caused him to leave the lipstick message on the wall. He might have killed again, in the case of Evelyn Peterson, if his attack had not been interrupted by a knock on the door. But did he kill Suzanne Degnan?

The abduction, murder and dismemberment of the little girl seemed to be a completely different method of murder than that used by the Lipstick Killer. While Heirens was certainly in the neighborhood around the time of the kidnapping, as evidenced by the burglary of the nearby apartment, this may have been merely a coincidence. There was little to link him to the crime, aside from a possible fingerprint on the ransom note and a knife that was found by reporters, not the police, and which could not be linked scientifically to the crime.

Heirens was not even the main suspect in the Degnan murder. Before he became a suspect, the police interrogated a forty-two-year-old drifter, Richard Russell Thomas, who was passing through the city at the time of the murder. Police handwriting experts noted the similarities between Thomas's handwriting and the ransom note. When questioned, he confessed to the murder, but he was released from custody after Heirens became the prime suspect.

In hindsight, it's very possible that Thomas might have been Degnan's killer. In addition to his handwriting possibly linking him to the murder, he had previously been convicted of attempted extortion, using a ransom note that threatened the kidnapping of a young girl. When he confessed to the crime, he was in jail awaiting sentencing for molesting his daughter. He had a history of violence, including spousal abuse. He was a nurse who sometimes posed as a surgeon and was known to steal surgical supplies, characteristics that matched the initial profile of the Degnan killer having surgical skills or being a butcher. Thomas also frequented a car agency near the Degnan residence, and parts of Suzanne's body were found in a sewer across the street from the agency.

Unfortunately, Chicago detectives dismissed Thomas's confession after Heirens was blamed for this crime, in addition to the Lipstick Murders. Thomas died in an Arizona prison in 1974. His prison record, and most of the evidence of his interrogation regarding the Degnan murder, has been either lost or destroyed.

Even if William Heirens did not kill Suzanne Degnan, he still deserved to go to prison for the assaults and burglaries that he confessed to. There was also no doubt that the Lipstick Murders came to an end after Heirens went to jail, which makes him the most likely suspect in those cases. His was a tragic case of a boy who went wrong at an early age, but he certainly made his own choices. He came from a good home, with loving parents, but he simply went the wrong direction somewhere along the way.

"Catch Me Before I Kill More"

As of this writing, William Heirens was eighty years old and had served sixty-two years in prison. He was the longest-serving prisoner in Illinois history. In 1998, he was transferred to the Dixon Correctional Center minimum security prison in Dixon, Illinois. He currently resides in the hospital ward and suffers from diabetes, which has limited his eyesight and forced him into a wheelchair.

In 2002, a petition was filed on Heirens's behalf seeking clemency. It not only cited doubts about his guilt but also his model behavior while in prison. The appeal was eventually denied. During a parole hearing in 2007, the board voted against parole. According to the *Suburban Chicago News*, a member of the Illinois Prisoner Review Board, Thomas Johnson, stated, "God will forgive you, but the state won't."

THE "NATURAL"
AND THE STALKER

Baseball players have had more than their share of female fans almost since the game began, but in some cases, fan adoration goes a little too far. This was exactly what happened to former Chicago Cubs first baseman Eddie Waitkus in 1949. He had no idea that a simple handwritten note, inviting him to a woman's hotel room, would have dire consequences that almost cost him his life.

Edward Waitkus was born in September 1919 in Cambridge, Massachusetts, and he loved baseball from an early age. He grew up in Boston, the son of Lithuanian immigrants, and started his professional career in 1938, playing for the Worumbo Indians, a semipro team that was sponsored by the Worumbo Woolen Mill in Lisbon Falls, Massachusetts. He enlisted in the army during World War II and saw some of the bloodiest fighting of the war in the Philippines, earning four Bronze Stars. When he returned to baseball, he quickly became a star for the Chicago Cubs and was a beloved figure in the newspapers and with the fans of the day. In 1918, he was traded to the Philadelphia Phillies for Dutch Leonard. He was elected to the National League All-Star team twice, in 1948 and 1949.

In June 1949, Waitkus returned to Chicago with the Phillies to play a series with the Cubs. He was only a few years into a very promising career, but fate was about to intervene in his life.

The Phillies stayed in Chicago at the Edgewater Beach Hotel, located at 5349 North Sheridan Road. The yellow-stuccoed building was the most elegant hotel on the North Side. With its famous Marine Room, which overlooked over one thousand yards of Lake Michigan beachfront, the hotel had opened in 1916 for the comfort and enjoyment of the upper class. Wealthy North Side residents quickly signed lease agreements for the Edgewater Beach Apartments, located in the residential annex at 5555 North Sheridan

Ballplayer Eddie Waitkus on the field.

Road, as soon as the development was announced. For years, partygoers had flocked to the Edgewater Beach for dinner, dancing and the music of Glenn Miller, Guy Lombardo and others.

The hotel was also frequently used by well-to-do travelers and baseball teams, like the Phillies, which played the Cubs at Wrigley Field. Nearly a month before Eddie Waitkus checked into the Edgewater Beach, a young Chicago woman named Ruth Steinhagen also reserved a room on the twelfth floor of the hotel. She would give anything to meet Eddie when he came back to town.

Although the two of them had never met, Ruth was madly in love with the former Cubs first baseman. At the age of only nineteen, she had fallen in love with Eddie two years before, when he was still playing in Chicago. She kept files of newspaper photographs of Waitkus and clipped stories in which he was mentioned. She sent protesting letters to the Cubs and to the newspapers when he was traded to Philadelphia. Alarmed at her behavior, her mother, Edith, urged her to see a psychiatrist. She saw two different doctors, but her infatuation with Eddie Waitkus continued. When her father, Walter, finally forbid her to mention Eddie's name in the house, Ruth became so upset that she moved out and took a small space in a rooming house at 1950 North Lincoln Avenue. It was reported that she kept a small private altar for Waitkus in her apartment. Ruth had fallen in love with Eddie when he was a Cub, but seeing him every day during the season apparently kept her feelings for him in check. Once he was traded to the Phillies and would only be back in Chicago for eleven games during the season, her obsession grew to dangerous proportions.

On Monday, June 13, Ruth checked into the Edgewater Beach Hotel, where she knew the Phillies would be staying. She brought with her a .22-caliber rifle, in two sections, which she had saved eighty dollars to buy. A friend, Helen Farazis, had gone with her to a North Avenue pawnshop to buy the gun, but she had believed Ruth when she said she needed it for protection. Farazis didn't explain to the police why she helped Ruth carry it to the hotel. According to the *Chicago Tribune*, Helen later told detectives that she had heard Ruth threaten several times to "get Eddie" but never took the threats seriously.

Ruth stayed in the hotel on Monday night but didn't try to get in touch with Waitkus until Tuesday evening. She ordered three drinks from room service and then paid a bellboy five dollars to deliver a note to Eddie's room. The note, which she had written some time earlier, was signed "Ruth Ann Burns," the name of an old schoolmate of Waitkus. According to the *Tribune*, it read:

> *It is extremely important that I see you as soon as possible. We're not acquainted, but I have something of importance to speak to you about. I think it would be to your advantage to let me explain this to you as I am leaving the hotel the day after tomorrow. I realize this is out of the ordinary, but as I say, this is extremely important.*

After sending the note, Ruth settled down to wait. She assembled her rifle and loaded it with one cartridge. As she waited, she later said that her desire to kill Waitkus came and went. After a few hours, when Eddie did not appear, Ruth went to bed. She was awakened about an hour later, however, by the telephone. Waitkus had received her note, and Ruth urged him to come up to her room but to wait a half hour so that she could get dressed. Waitkus, probably assuming that he was about to be treated to a late-night assignation with an adoring fan, readily agreed.

At about 11:20 p.m., Eddie knocked on the door and introduced himself. As Eddie walked over to a chair and sat down, Ruth went to the closet to get her rifle. "I have a surprise for you," she said, pointing the gun at the startled ballplayer.

"Here, what's this all about?" Waitkus cried.

Ruth answered by making him get up out of his chair and move toward the window.

"For two years you've been bothering me and now you're going to die," Ruth said.

The Edgewater Beach Hotel in a 1933 postcard of Chicago.

A newspaper photo of Ruth Ann Steinhagen behind bars after the shooting of Eddie Waitkus. *Courtesy of the* Chicago Daily News.

The "Natural" and the Stalker

Waitkus was still confused. "What in the world goes on here?"

Ruth's reply came from the barrel of the rifle. She fired a single shot into Eddie's chest, and he fell to the floor and rolled onto his back. "Baby, what did you do this for?" he choked out.

Ruth knelt beside him and held onto his hand. He managed to smile up at her, likely in confusion and perhaps even unaware that he was bleeding into the carpet. "You like this, don't you?" he asked her, still smiling oddly. "But why in the name of heaven did you do this to me?"

Ruth didn't answer. At this point, her plan had been to shoot herself, she later said, but she didn't have the courage. Instead, she called the hotel operator and stated that she had just shot a man in her room. Hotel Detective Edward Purdy and the hotel's physician, Dr. Andrew Dick, hurried to her room. Purdy turned Ruth over to the custody of police officers at the Summerdale district station. Waitkus, meanwhile, was rushed to the Illinois Masonic Hospital, where doctors immediately took him into surgery. The *Chicago Tribune* reported that Dr. L.L. Braun, one of his attending physicians, described the player's condition as "fair to poor and critical" and announced that it was "touch and go as to whether he'll live."

Ruth was questioned for several hours by the police and charged with assault with intent to murder. She said that she wanted to do away with Eddie Waitkus because she wanted something exciting in her life. She had taken a job as a typist for a Michigan Avenue insurance company after moving out of her parent's house. "I didn't want to go back to typing," Ruth told the *Tribune.* "I didn't want to live like that." As detectives spoke with her parents and friends, they began to discover Ruth's obsession with Eddie Waitkus, likely caused by some sort of mental instability.

Five operations were needed to restore Eddie's health, and he spent nearly a month in the hospital, but he survived. In fact, he was back on the field for the 1950 season and was named Comeback Player of the Year, helping the Phillies win the pennant. Eddie stayed with the Phillies until 1953, when he was traded to the Baltimore Orioles. He returned to Philadelphia for his final season in 1955.

Eddie Waitkus may have walked away from the shooting in good physical health, but it did its damage psychologically. He suffered from post-traumatic stress as a result of it, which ultimately affected both his career and his marriage. But his final years were satisfying to him, as he became an instructor for Ted Williams's baseball camp, an activity he enjoyed and one that he continued almost to the end of his life. Eddie Waitkus died from cancer in 1972.

Author Bernard Malamud, who was a baseball fan, took the basic elements of the Waitkus shooting and wove them into a novel, a morality tale called *The Natural*. The book was released in 1952 and was eventually made into a film that was released in 1984. The title came from the fact that during Waitkus's rookie year, sports writers often referred to the young man as "a natural." The novel ended tragically and unknowingly foreshadowed Waitkus's own downfall as a player a few years later.

On June 30, Ruth Steinhagen appeared in court and was indicted, found to be insane by a jury and committed to the Kankakee State Hospital, all in the same day. Over the course of the next three years, Ruth responded well to electroshock therapy and was released on April 17, 1952—less than three years after shooting Eddie Waitkus.

Eddie and Ruth never met again, but years later, Waitkus still had vivid recollections of the young woman. According to C. Philip Frances in "The Eddie Waitkus Affair," Waitkus commented, "She had the coldest-looking face that I ever saw."

BIBLIOGRAPHY

Adler, Jeffrey S. *First in Violence, Deepest in Dirt*. Cambridge, MA: Harvard University Press, 2006.

Asbury, Herbert. *Gem of the Prairie*. New York: Alfred A. Knopf, 1940.

Bilek, Arthur J. *The First Vice Lord*. Nashville, TN: Cumberland House, 2008.

Chicago Historical Society

Chicago Public Library

Cowdery, Ray. *Capone's Chicago*. Lakeville, MN: Northstar Commemoratives, 1987.

Demaris, Ovid. *Captive City* New York: Lyle Stuart, 1969.

Farr, Finis. *Chicago*. New Rochelle, NY: Arlington House, 1973.

Francis, C. Philip. "The Eddie Waitkus Affair." http://www.chatterfromthedugout.com/eddie_waitkus_affair.htm.

Halper, Albert. *The Chicago Crime Book*. Cleveland, OH: World Publishing, 1967.

Helmer, William. *Public Enemies*. New York: Facts on File, 1998.

BIBLIOGRAPHY

Helmer, William, and Arthur J. Bilek. *The St. Valentine's Day Massacre*. Nashville, TN: Cumberland House, 2004.

Johnson, Curt, with R. Craig Sautter. *Wicked City*. Highland Park, IL: December Press, 1994.

Keefe, Rose. *Guns and Roses*. Nashville, TN: Cumberland House, 2003.

————. *The Man Who Got Away*. Nashville, TN: Cumberland House, 2005.

King, Jeffrey S. *Rise and Fall of the Dillinger Gang*. Nashville, TN: Cumberland House, 2005.

Kobler, John. *Capone*. New York: G.P. Putnam's Sons, 1971.

Lait, Jack, and Lee Mortimer. *Chicago Confidential*. New York: Crown Publishers, 1950.

Landesco, John. *Organized Crime in Chicago*. Chicago: University of Chicago Press, 1968.

Lesy, Michael. *Murder City*. New York: W.W. Norton & Co., 2007.

Lewis, Lloyd, and Henry Justin Smith. *Chicago*. New York: Harcourt, Brace & Co., 1929.

Lindberg, Richard. *Chicago by Gaslight*. Chicago: Chicago Academy Publishers, 1996.

————. *Return Again to the Scene of the Crime*. Nashville, TN: Cumberland House, 2001.

————. *Return to the Scene of the Crime*. Nashville, TN: Cumberland House, 1999.

Loerzel, Robert. *Alchemy of Bones*. Urbana: University of Illinois Press, 2003.

Matera, Dary. *John Dillinger*. New York: Carroll & Graf, 2004.

BIBLIOGRAPHY

McPhaul, Jack. *Johnny Torrio: First of the Ganglords*. New Rochelle, NY: Arlington House, 1970.

"The Monster that Terrorized Chicago." http://home.earthlink.net/~chicago1946/.

Nash, Jay Robert. *Bloodletters and Bad Men*. New York: M. Evans and Company, Inc., 1995.

————. *Open Files*. New York: McGraw-Hill Book Co., 1983.

Shmelter, Richard J. *Chicago Assassin*. Nashville, TN: Cumberland House, 2008.

Sifakis, Carl. *Encyclopedia of American Crime*. New York: Facts on File, 1982.

Taylor, Troy. *Bloody Chicago*. Decatur, IL: Whitechapel Press, 2006.

————. *Bloody Illinois*. Decatur, IL: Whitechapel Press, 2008.

————. *Dead Men Do Tell Tales*. Decatur, IL: Whitechapel Press, 2008.

Toland, John. *Dillinger Days*. New York: Da Capo Press, 1995.

Wright, Sewell Peaslee. *Chicago Murders*. New York: Duell, Sloan & Pierce, 1945.

NEWSPAPERS

Chicago American
Chicago Daily News
Chicago Herald-American
Chicago Herald & Examiner
Chicago Inter-Ocean
Chicago Sun-Times
Chicago Times
Chicago Tribune

ABOUT THE AUTHOR

Troy Taylor is the author of more than sixty books on history, crime, mysteries and the supernatural in America. He was born and raised in Illinois and currently resides in Decatur, Illinois, which was called "one of the most corrupt cities in the state" during the 1920s.

Visit us at
www.historypress.net